I0605568

Bake It Gluten Free

Bake It Gluten Free

100 RECIPES FOR CLASSIC TREATS

DANA POLLACK
WITH DEVON O'BRIEN

Photographs by Morgan Ione Yeager

UNION SQUARE & CO.
NEW YORK

UNION SQUARE & CO. and the distinctive Union Square & Co. logo are trademarks of Hachette Book Group, Inc.

ISBN 978-1-4549-5656-3
ISBN 978-1-4549-5657-0 (e-book)

Union Square & Co. books may be purchased in bulk for business, educational, or promotional use. For more information, please contact your local bookseller or the Hachette Book Group's Special Markets department at special.markets@hbgusa.com.

Printed in China

10 9 8 7 6 5 4 3 2 1

unionsquareandco.com

Editor: Caitlin Leffel
Designer: Renée Bollier
Photographer: Morgan Ione Yeager
Food Stylist: Judy Haubert
Prop Stylist: Ashleigh Sarbone
Project Editor: Ivy McFadden
Production Manager: Kevin Iwano

Additional image credit:
Page 13: Shutterstock.com/Ithile

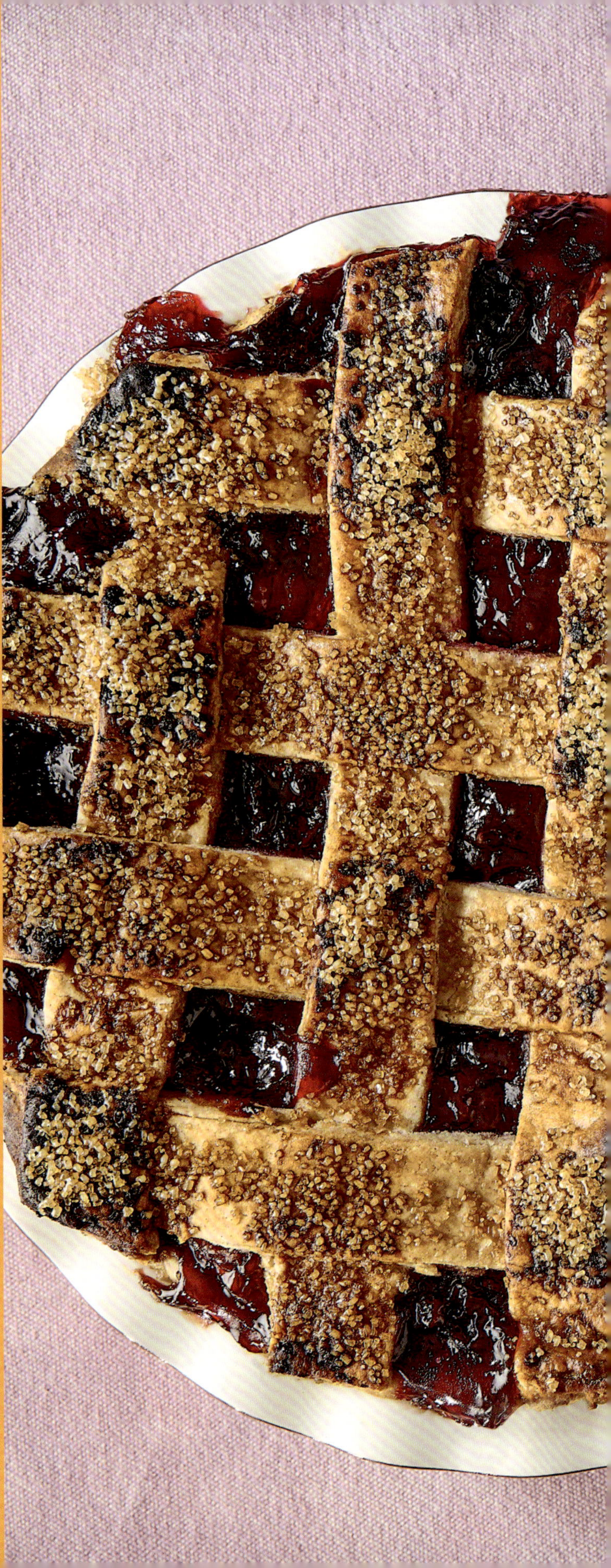

Leni and Ella,
as is everything,
this book is for you xx

CONTENTS

Introduction 9
Gluten-Free Guide 11
Substitutions 15

Cookies

19 Strawberry Shortcake Cookies
20 Stuffed Fluffernutter Cookies
23 Cosmic No-Bake Cookies
24 Black & White Cookies
27 Dark Chocolate Sandwich Cookies
28 Lucky Charms Cereal Cookies
31 Rocky Road Cookies
32 Mandel Bread
35 Chocolate Espresso Cookies
36 Cake Batter Macarons
39 Oatmeal Raisin Cookies
40 Crispy Chocolate Chip Cookies
43 Confetti Shortbread Cookies
44 Cut-Out Sugar Cookies
47 Chocolate-Covered Strawberry Macarons

Cakes

51 Red Velvet Cake
52 Confetti Birthday Cake
55 Strawberries & Cream Cake
56 Flourless Peanut Butter–Chocolate Mug Cake
59 Tiramisu Trifle
61 Carrot Cake
65 Upside-Down Bananas Foster Cake
66 Dirt Cup Poke Cake
69 Raspberry Swirl Cheesecake
70 Neapolitan Bundt Cake
73 Chocolate Layer Cake

Breads

77 Chocolate Swirl Pumpkin Bread
78 Soft Pretzels
81 Chocolate Babka
83 Cinnamon Morning Buns
87 Babka French Toast
88 Challah Bread Pudding
91 Zucchini Bread
92 Pull-Apart Cinnamon Bread
95 Speedy Bagels
96 Challah
99 Croissants
101 Sourdough Bread
105 Cranberry-Orange Scones
106 Apple Cinnamon Baked Oats

Bars

111 Rainbow Chocolate Chip Granola Bars
112 S'mores Brownies
115 Scotcheroos
116 Brown Butter Rice Crispy Treats
119 Oreo Cheesecake Bars
120 Frosted Sugar Cookie Bars
123 Cheesecake Swirl Brownies
124 Chocolate Chunk Brown Butter Blondies
127 Peach Crumble Bars
128 Chocolate Mint Brownies

Cupcakes

133 Strawberry Cheesecake Cupcakes
134 Cookies & Cream Cupcakes
137 Lemon Cupcakes
139 Cream-Filled Chocolate Cupcakes
141 Crème Brûlée Cupcakes
145 White Cake Cupcakes
146 Chocolate Zucchini Cupcakes
149 Cannoli Cones
150 Sweet Potato Cinnamon Cupcakes
153 Boston Cream Cupcakes
155 Millionaire's Cupcakes

Pies

161 Stone Fruit Galette
162 Sour Cherry Pie
165 Frangipane Fruit Tart
166 Chocolate Fluffernutter Pie
169 Coconut Caramel Chocolate Pie
170 Red Wine Pear Tart
173 Lemon Poppy Seed Tart
174 Apple & Brie Galette
177 Skillet Blueberry Crumble
178 Grandma Doris's Apple Pie
181 Chocolate Pecan Pie

Ice Cream

187 Nutella Fudge Pops
188 Cookies & Cream Ice Cream
191 Banana Split Pudding Pops
192 Red Velvet Ice Cream
195 Pineapple Whip
196 Rainbow Sherbet
199 Orange Sorbet
200 No-Churn Coffee Ice Cream
203 Ice Cream Sandwiches
207 Brownie Batter Ice Cream
208 Cookie Dough Ice Cream

Donuts

213 Apple Fritters
214 Chocolate Donut Holes
217 Lemon Ricotta Donuts
218 Glazed Crullers
221 Nutella-Stuffed Beignets
222 Cinnamon-Sugar Yeast-Risen Baked Donuts
225 Baked Chocolate-Glazed Donuts
226 Stuffed Churros
229 DOH!nuts

Acknowledgments 232
Index 234

INTRODUCTION

FLASHBACK TO 2010, Midtown New York City, and I'm a photo editor at *Muscle & Fitness* magazine. Sitting in my cubicle, staring at photos of men in Speedos from my most recent shoot, I realized this was not my calling. It was highly entertaining, to say the least, but I realized something was missing—passion. But what did I love to do? What made *me* happy enough that I could do it every day and not get bored? What was I *already* doing every day or looking forward to doing that was filling my cup? Then the lightbulb went off:

Baking.

Baking, cooking, and entertaining has always been my love language. Even as a little girl, I would host "dinner parties" for my stuffed animals, and when I grew up, I graduated to making real meals for my family and friends. It's how I show someone I care for them, and it's how I care for myself, the ultimate stress-reliever. And it hit me—I could actually turn this passion into a living. That's when what I coin "the sweet life" started—within two weeks of this realization, I quit my job and enrolled in culinary school. Little did I know, it would get even sweeter when I eventually opened Dana's Bakery.

I've mastered gluten-free baking, and for over a decade, I've catered to our customers with dietary restrictions. So I know being gluten-intolerant doesn't have to mean missing out on your favorite baked goods. I've taken classic desserts and given them the Dana's spin (think fun, vibrant, and playful), making them gluten-free without sacrificing any creativity or flavor. Even my two picky eaters (my daughters, Leni and Ella) were so excited to eat (and better yet, to help me make) all the recipes in this book. So I promise, even your gluten-loving friends will be coming back for seconds.

In my more than twelve years of creating gluten-free goodies for Dana's Bakery, I've learned all the best tricks of the trade to easily make delicious gluten-free baked goods, and I've folded all those tricks into the recipes in this book. YES, it is *finally* possible to make the cinnamon buns (page 83) you've been craving or that loaf of challah (page 88) you've been missing at Shabbat dinner. And don't even get me started on the entire cake chapter (see pages 51–73). I really did make something for everyone, so let's get baking!

GLUTEN-FREE GUIDE

Baking gluten-free is a totally different beast from baking with traditional wheat flour, but it doesn't have to be scary. These tips will make you a pro in no time.

Key Ingredients

You'll see **gluten-free 1:1 replacement flour blend** called for in almost every recipe in this book, and for good reason! Instead of stocking my pantry with a grocery store's worth of different types of gluten-free flours, I like to keep just one all-purpose blend on hand to use in everything I make. There are a lot of great ones on the market from brands like King Arthur and Cup4Cup, but of course my favorite is our proprietary Dana's Bakery gluten-free flour blend (you can find it at select stores or online at DanasBakery.com).

Flour blends containing **gluten-free wheat starch** are on the rise. It may sound like an oxymoron, because gluten is the protein found in wheat, but since the wheat starch doesn't contain any wheat proteins, it's gluten-free. (Given that it's derived from wheat, though, this ingredient is still a no-go if you have a wheat allergy.) Caputo, an Italian brand, has a popular gluten-free flour blend containing wheat starch that makes superb pizza and breads, but now there are US brands using it, too (and it's FDA-approved!). Try swapping it in for regular gluten-free flour blend in the bread recipes in the book, like the Sourdough (page 101), Soft Pretzels (page 78), Croissants (page 99), Challah (page 96), and Chocolate Babka (page 81). Just skip the psyllium husk listed in the recipes, since these blends already contain it.

Speaking of **psyllium husk**—that's another ingredient you'll see in a lot of the bread recipes in this book. It plays a key role in gluten-free baking, as it mimics the stretchiness of gluten, strengthening the dough so it's able to trap more air and get a good rise while baking. An added bonus? Psyllium husk is pretty much pure fiber, giving your baked goods a little nutritional boost. It comes in two forms: whole or ground. Ground husks are best for baking. Look for it in the supplement section of the grocery store or health food stores (you can also order it online). But as I found during testing the recipes for this book, not all brands are created equal. The ones I found work the best are Anthony's, Viva Naturals, and Organic India.

When shopping for **oats**, don't forget to look for certified gluten-free brands. The way conventional oats are grown and processed introduces a lot of opportunities for cross contamination, so you want to make sure you are getting oats that are completely gluten-free.

Similarly, when reaching for a **crisped rice cereal**, check the label for that gluten-free certification. Believe it or not, Kellogg's Rice Krispies are not gluten-free because they contain barley malt. My favorite cereal brand to use is Malt-O-Meal. They have a variety of certified-GF cereals like plain crispies, cocoa crispies, and even fruity cereal.

The 6 Rules of Gluten-Free Baking

1

Just buy a kitchen scale. OK, to be fair: It isn't always necessary. But if you want to get into making gluten-free bread like the sourdough on page 101 or the cinnamon buns on page 83, measuring ingredients by weight instead of volume is going to be more accurate and give you more consistent results every time. Plus, you can place your bowl on the scale and measure everything directly in it (just don't forget to tare, or zero out, the scale between ingredients)—no more washing all those measuring cups and spoons!

2

Don't rise like you used to. You may notice that some of these recipes have short initial rise times or skip a first rise before shaping—that's not an accident. Traditionally, the first rise in yeasted doughs is to help gluten formation before shaping the dough for a strong rise later. But since there isn't any gluten to form here, that initial rise is not necessary, and the more air you push out of a dough early in the process, the less you will have later. So often I will shape a dough right after mixing it to make sure all that air stays trapped for better rise while baking.

3

Get rid of the grit. Grittiness in gluten-free goods is common, but more often than not, it's because of the flour blend you are using. If you find that your baked goods are coming out sandy or gritty, try letting your doughs and batters hydrate. Letting them sit for even just 10 minutes can help the dough fully hydrate, creating a better texture. Hydration time is also very important for gluten-free doughs containing psyllium husk, as it has to soak up a lot of moisture before it mimics gluten. This is why, despite rule #2, some of my bread recipes still call for an initial rise time.

4

Don't be afraid to knead. While you don't need to knead gluten-free doughs as much as gluten-containing ones (more on that in a minute), you also don't need to be afraid to knead them either. GF doughs tend to be more delicate, but if you are finding your bread and doughnut doughs to be too sticky to shape, go ahead and knead, adding extra flour a little at a time, until the dough is smooth and firm enough to shape as desired.

5

Whip it real good. One of the beauties of gluten-free baking is just that: There is no gluten! This means you don't have to fold dough every 20 minutes for a whole day (I'm looking at you, sourdough) or knead it until your arms go numb. But it also means you don't have to worry about tender baked goods like cakes and cookies getting too tough from too much gluten development. In other words, you can't overmix gluten-free batter, and you are therefore more likely to get baked goods that are more tender and moist than you would if you were baking with gluten. So go ahead and whip that cake batter until it's light and airy.

6

Line that pan! You'll notice I call for parchment paper in almost every recipe. This is crucial in helping you easily remove your baked goods from their pans without any cracks or rips, which delicate gluten-free bakes are especially prone to. When it comes to cupcakes, muffin cup liners are your best friend. Without them, gluten-free cupcakes tend to fall and become more dense—which, for something like the Cream-Filled Chocolate Cupcakes on page 139, is actually good and why I don't call for them in that recipe, but for all the others in this book, stick with using liners.

SUBSTITUTIONS

Buttermilk

No **buttermilk**? No problem! Just combine ¼ cup milk with 1 teaspoon distilled white vinegar or fresh lemon juice to use in its place.

Eggs & Egg Whites

When it comes to swapping out **eggs**, there is no one substitute that's great for all applications. For cakes, swap in 3 tablespoons coconut flour mixed with 1 tablespoon water for each large egg. For cookies, I like a combination of 3 tablespoons flax meal mixed with 1 tablespoon water. If you're swapping out **egg whites**, opt for 3 tablespoons aquafaba (the liquid from a can of chickpeas) for each large white. And in place of an **egg wash**, simply use milk or cream instead.

Dairy

If you're looking to make these recipes vegan, swap in your favorite nut milk for cow's **milk**, and swap out the **butter** for a plant-based version. I love Miyoko's Creamery plant milk butter, but Earth Balance is an easy-to-find substitute that always works.

Sugar

Don't forget: To make these recipes vegan, you will need to sub in organic sugar. Conventional sugar can be processed using animal products, but organic sugar is entirely plant-based from start to finish. If the recipe calls for **honey**, swap in maple syrup instead.

COOKIES

Strawberry Shortcake Cookies

Makes
12 cookies

Strawberry shortcake doesn't always have to be a cake—it's just as good in cookie form. Some people (hi, Leni!) may even argue that it's way better that way! These are best eaten on the day they're baked, so if you want to save some for another day, store the frozen cookie dough balls in an airtight container in your freezer for up to three months. That way, you can pull some out to bake whenever the craving strikes!

- 1½ cups (210 grams) gluten-free 1:1 replacement flour blend
- ½ teaspoon baking powder
- ½ teaspoon kosher salt
- ¼ teaspoon baking soda
- ½ cup (1 stick) unsalted butter, melted
- ½ cup (100 grams) granulated sugar
- ¼ cup packed (55 grams) light brown sugar
- 1 large egg
- 1 teaspoon pure vanilla extract
- 1 cup (165 grams) diced fresh strawberries

1 Line a baking sheet with parchment paper.

2 In a medium bowl, whisk together the flour, baking powder, salt, and baking soda.

3 In a large bowl, whisk together the melted butter, granulated sugar, and brown sugar until combined. Add the egg and vanilla and whisk until smooth. Gradually stir in the dry ingredients until just combined. Gently fold in the strawberries until just combined.

4 Using a 3-tablespoon scoop, scoop the dough onto the prepared baking sheet, spacing the cookies 1 inch apart. Freeze until firm, at least 1 hour, or transfer to an airtight container and freeze for up to 3 months.

5 Preheat the oven to 350°F.

6 Bake the cookies for about 25 minutes, until the tops are lightly golden. Remove from the oven and let cool before eating, about 1 hour. These are best eaten the same day.

Stuffed Fluffernutter Cookies

Makes
16 cookies

I'm ready to make Marshmallow Fluff cool again! If you were a peanut-butter-and-Fluff-sandwich lover as a kid, you know what I'm talking about—the sweet and creamy marshmallow pairs perfectly with the salty peanut butter for an ooey-gooey masterpiece. This is that sandwich in cookie form. Freezing the dough after stuffing it with the Fluff ensures that the Fluff stays creamy in the center and doesn't melt away in the oven.

1½ cups (210 grams) gluten-free 1:1 replacement flour blend

1 teaspoon baking powder

½ teaspoon baking soda

½ teaspoon kosher salt

½ cup (1 stick) unsalted butter, at room temperature

¾ cup packed (160 grams) light brown sugar

¾ cup (150 grams) granulated sugar

1 cup (255 grams) creamy peanut butter

2 large eggs, at room temperature

1 teaspoon pure vanilla extract

1 cup (130 grams) Marshmallow Fluff

1 Line two baking sheets with parchment paper.

2 In a medium bowl, whisk together the flour, baking powder, baking soda, and salt.

3 In the bowl of a stand mixer fitted with the paddle attachment, combine the butter, brown sugar, and granulated sugar and beat on medium-low speed until smooth, about 2 minutes. Add the peanut butter, eggs, and vanilla and beat until smooth. Gradually beat in the dry ingredients until fully incorporated.

4 Using a 3-tablespoon scoop, portion the dough onto the prepared baking sheets, spacing the cookies at least 2 inches apart. Flatten each portion, then place 1 tablespoon of the Fluff in the center and wrap the dough around it to encase it. Freeze until solid, about 1 hour.

5 Preheat the oven to 350°F.

6 Bake one sheet at a time for about 15 minutes, until the cookies are brown around the edges. Remove from the oven and let cool completely, about 1 hour. Repeat with the remaining baking sheet. Store in an airtight container at room temperature for up to 3 days.

Cosmic No-Bake Cookies

Makes
20 cookies

Rainbow chips give these cookies the look and flavor of a Cosmic Brownie, but they're way easier (and faster) to make—you don't even have to turn on your oven. You can find rainbow chips online, but if you don't have them on hand, feel free to mix in your favorite sprinkles or small candies like mini M&M's, peanut butter chips, or even dried cranberries or cherries.

- ½ cup (1 stick) unsalted butter
- ½ cup (115 grams) whole milk
- 1 cup (170 grams) semisweet chocolate chips
- ¼ cup (90 grams) honey
- 3 cups (375 grams) gluten-free quick-cooking oats
- ¼ teaspoon kosher salt
- ½ cup (85 grams) rainbow chocolate chips, plus more for sprinkling

1 Line a baking sheet with parchment paper.

2 In a large saucepan, combine the butter and milk. Heat over medium-high heat, stirring continuously, until melted and combined, about 5 minutes. Bring the mixture to a boil, stirring continuously, then remove from the heat. Add the chocolate chips and honey and stir until melted and combined. Add the oats and salt and stir until the oats are thoroughly coated in the liquid. Stir in the rainbow chips.

3 Scoop 2-tablespoon mounds of the dough onto the prepared baking sheet, spacing the cookies 1 inch apart. Use your fingers to flatten each into a 2-inch round. Top each cookie with a sprinkle of rainbow chips, pressing them into the cookies to adhere. Refrigerate until firm before serving, at least 30 minutes, or transfer to an airtight container and refrigerate for up to 3 days.

Black & White Cookies

Makes 12 cookies

There is nothing better than a classic New York black & white cookie (even Jerry Seinfeld agrees). It's hard to find a good gluten-free one, so naturally, when we launched them at Dana's Bakery, they became one of our bestsellers. The cookie is soft and fluffy—almost cakey—and the icing on top adds just the right amount of sweetness. You're always welcome to order them from us, but now you can make them at home, too!

COOKIES

2¼ cups (310 grams) gluten-free 1:1 replacement flour blend

1 teaspoon baking powder

½ teaspoon kosher salt

½ cup (1 stick) unsalted butter, at room temperature

1½ cups (300 grams) granulated sugar

2 large eggs, at room temperature

1 teaspoon pure vanilla extract

½ cup (85 grams) buttermilk

ICING

3 cups (340 grams) powdered sugar

2 tablespoons light corn syrup

½ teaspoon pure vanilla extract

2 tablespoons unsweetened cocoa powder

1 **Make the cookies:** Preheat the oven to 350°F. Line two large baking sheets with parchment paper.

2 In a medium bowl, whisk together the flour, baking powder, and salt.

3 In the bowl of a stand mixer fitted with the paddle attachment, beat the butter and granulated sugar on medium speed until light and fluffy, 3 to 5 minutes. Beat in the eggs one at a time until smooth. Beat in the vanilla. Add the dry ingredients in three additions, alternating with the buttermilk, and beat until smooth.

4 Using a heaping ⅓-cup scoop, portion the dough onto the prepared baking sheets, spacing the cookies 2 inches apart. Bake for about 17 minutes, until lightly golden. Remove from the oven and let cool on the baking sheets for 10 minutes, then transfer to a wire rack to cool completely, about 1 hour.

5 **Make the icing:** In a large bowl, whisk together the powdered sugar, corn syrup, vanilla, and 2 tablespoons water until smooth.

6 Flip the cookies so they are flat-side up and coat half of each cookie with the icing. Let set until the icing is dry to the touch, about 30 minutes.

7 Meanwhile, stir the cocoa powder and 1 tablespoon water into the icing remaining in the bowl. Coat the opposite half of each cookie with the chocolate icing. Let set until the icing is dry to the touch, about 30 minutes. Store in an airtight container at room temperature for up to 3 days.

Dark Chocolate Sandwich Cookies

Makes about
24 sandwich cookies

Milanos were one of my favorite cookies when I was growing up. So when I started baking, learning how to make them was a *must*! Once I mastered that, I wanted to make a gluten-free version for you all. Feel free to make these as is, or get creative and put your own spin on the classic cookie by adding orange zest or peppermint oil to the melted chocolate.

1 cup (140 grams) gluten-free 1:1 replacement flour blend

¼ teaspoon baking powder

¼ teaspoon kosher salt

½ cup (1 stick) unsalted butter, at room temperature

½ cup (100 grams) sugar

2 large eggs

1 teaspoon pure vanilla extract

2 tablespoons whole milk

1 cup (170 grams) bittersweet chocolate chips

1 Preheat the oven to 350°F. Line two baking sheets with parchment paper.

2 In a medium bowl, whisk together the flour, baking powder, and salt.

3 In the bowl of a stand mixer fitted with the paddle attachment, beat the butter and sugar on medium speed until light and fluffy, about 2 minutes. Add the eggs one at a time and beat until smooth, about 1 minute. Beat in the vanilla. With the mixer running, add the dry ingredients in three additions, alternating with the milk, and mix until combined and smooth, about 1 minute.

4 Transfer the batter to a large zip-top bag and snip one corner off, creating a ½-inch hole. Pipe the batter onto the prepared baking sheets in 2×1-inch ovals.

5 Bake one sheet at a time for about 18 minutes, until the edges are lightly browned, rotating the pan from front to back halfway through. Remove from the oven and let cool completely, about 30 minutes. Repeat with the second baking sheet.

6 Place the chocolate chips in a medium microwave-safe bowl and microwave in 30-second intervals, stirring after each, until melted and smooth.

7 Using a small rubber spatula or spoon, spread the melted chocolate over the flat side of half the cookies. Sandwich the filling with the remaining cookies, flat-side down. Let stand until the chocolate has hardened, about 1 hour. Store in an airtight container at room temperature for up to 4 days.

Lucky Charms Cereal Cookies

Makes 16 cookies

Over the past decade, General Mills has slowly made some of its most popular cereals gluten-free—including Lucky Charms. I love using them for crispy bars (try them in place of the crisped rice cereal in the recipe on page 116), but they're also great in cookies. The toasted cereal pieces grind up into a flavorful powder that I use in place of some of the flour in this recipe. Not only does it add flavor, it also makes the cookies light and crisp. I press the marshmallows on top of the dough balls rather than mixing them in so they hold their shape better for the perfect look.

- 2 cups (70 grams) Lucky Charms cereal
- 2 cups (275 grams) gluten-free 1:1 replacement flour blend
- ¾ teaspoon baking powder
- ½ teaspoon kosher salt
- 1 cup (2 sticks) unsalted butter, melted
- 1 cup (200 grams) granulated sugar
- ½ cup packed (105 grams) light brown sugar
- 2 large eggs, at room temperature
- 1 teaspoon pure vanilla extract

1 Preheat the oven to 350°F. Line two baking sheets with parchment paper.

2 Separate the marshmallows from the cereal pieces in the Lucky Charms, placing the cereal pieces in a food processor. Process until the cereal pieces are ground into a fine powder, then transfer to a medium bowl and whisk in the flour, baking powder, and salt.

3 In a large bowl, whisk together the melted butter, granulated sugar, and brown sugar until combined. Whisk in the eggs and vanilla until smooth. Add the dry ingredients to the wet ingredients one-third at a time, stirring until each addition is fully incorporated before adding the next.

4 Using a 3-tablespoon scoop, portion the dough onto the prepared baking sheets, spacing the cookies at least 2 inches apart. Distribute the Lucky Charms marshmallows among the dough balls, pressing them in lightly to adhere.

5 Bake one sheet at a time for about 14 minutes, until the cookies are golden on the edges. Remove from the oven and let cool completely, about 1 hour. Repeat with the remaining baking sheet. Store in an airtight container at room temperature for up to 3 days.

Rocky Road Cookies

Makes 12 cookies

Rocky road is classically a mixture of marshmallows, nuts, and chocolates, but if you have a nut allergy, simply omit the almonds. If you're not a fan of almonds, swap them out for another nut such as peanuts, pecans, or even pistachios.

- 1 cup (140 grams) gluten-free 1:1 replacement flour blend
- 1 tablespoon unsweetened cocoa powder
- ½ teaspoon baking powder
- ¼ teaspoon baking soda
- ¼ teaspoon kosher salt
- 1 cup (170 grams) bittersweet chocolate chips
- ½ cup (1 stick) unsalted butter
- ⅓ cup packed (70 grams) light brown sugar
- ⅓ cup (65 grams) granulated sugar
- 1 large egg
- 1 teaspoon pure vanilla extract
- 1 cup (55 grams) mini marshmallows
- ½ cup (60 grams) sliced almonds

1 Line two baking sheets with parchment paper.

2 In a medium bowl, whisk together the flour, cocoa powder, baking powder, baking soda, and salt.

3 Place ½ cup of the chocolate chips and the butter in a medium microwave-safe bowl and microwave in 30-second intervals, stirring after each, until completely melted and smooth. Add the brown sugar and granulated sugar and whisk thoroughly to combine. Whisk in the egg and vanilla until smooth.

4 Add the dry ingredients to the chocolate mixture one-third at a time, stirring until fully incorporated after each addition. Fold in the remaining ½ cup chocolate chips, the marshmallows, and the almonds.

5 Using a 3-tablespoon scoop, portion the dough onto the prepared baking sheets, spacing the cookies at least 2 inches apart. Freeze until firm, about 1 hour.

6 Preheat the oven to 350°F.

7 Bake one sheet at a time for about 14 minutes, until set. Remove from the oven and let cool completely, about 1 hour. Repeat with the remaining baking sheet. Store in an airtight container at room temperature for up to 3 days.

Mandel Bread

Makes about 15 cookies

Mandel bread comes from the Yiddish word for the cookie: *mandelbrot*, literally meaning "almond bread." It's a twice-baked cookie flavored with almond and often studded with chocolate chips and/or dried fruit (I prefer chocolate chips alone). Yes, it looks like biscotti, but the texture is softer and denser. Plus, it's made with oil instead of butter, making it dairy-free.

- 2 cups (275 grams) gluten-free 1:1 replacement flour blend
- 1 teaspoon baking powder
- ¼ teaspoon kosher salt
- ¾ cup (150 grams) sugar
- ½ cup (100 grams) neutral oil, such as avocado, sunflower, grapeseed, or canola oil
- 2 large eggs
- 1 teaspoon pure vanilla extract
- ½ teaspoon pure almond extract
- ½ cup (90 grams) dairy-free mini chocolate chips
- ½ teaspoon ground cinnamon

1 Preheat the oven to 350°F. Line a baking sheet with parchment paper.

2 In a medium bowl, whisk together the flour, baking powder, and salt.

3 In a large bowl, whisk together ½ cup (100 grams) of the sugar, the oil, eggs, vanilla, and almond extract until smooth. Stir the dry ingredients into the wet ingredients, then fold in the chocolate chips.

4 Turn the dough out onto the prepared baking sheet and form it into an 8 × 4-inch mound. Bake for about 25 minutes, until browned. Remove from the oven and let cool until cool enough to handle, about 30 minutes. Keep the oven on.

5 Meanwhile, in a shallow bowl, combine the remaining ¼ cup (50 grams) sugar and the cinnamon.

6 Transfer the loaf to a cutting board and cut it crosswise into ½-inch-thick slices. Dip each slice in the cinnamon-sugar mixture, turning to coat, then return them to the baking sheet, cut-side down. Bake for about 20 minutes more, until golden. Remove from the oven and let cool completely, about 30 minutes, before serving or storing.

7 Store in an airtight container at room temperature for up to 3 days.

Chocolate Espresso Cookies

Makes
12 cookies

As anyone who follows me on Instagram knows, I can't live without my morning coffee. It puts the pep in my step to get me through my busy days running a bakery and parenting two kids, but I also adore the flavor. Any excuse to get a second dose of coffee is good enough for me, and these cookies are just the ticket. Espresso powder gives these all the delicious coffee flavor with a fraction of the caffeine so you can enjoy one any time of day.

- 2 cups (275 grams) gluten-free 1:1 replacement flour blend
- 2 tablespoons unsweetened cocoa powder
- 1 teaspoon baking powder
- 1 teaspoon espresso powder
- ½ teaspoon baking soda
- ½ teaspoon kosher salt
- 1⅓ cups (225 grams) chocolate chips, melted
- 1 cup (2 sticks) unsalted butter
- ¾ cup packed (160 grams) light brown sugar
- ¾ cup (150 grams) granulated sugar
- 2 large eggs
- 2 teaspoons pure vanilla extract

1 Line two baking sheets with parchment paper.

2 In a medium bowl, whisk together the flour, cocoa powder, baking powder, espresso powder, baking soda, and salt.

3 Place the chocolate chips and butter in a medium microwave-safe bowl and microwave in 30-second intervals, stirring after each, until completely melted and smooth. Add the brown sugar and granulated sugar and whisk thoroughly to combine. Whisk in the eggs and vanilla until smooth. Fold in the dry ingredients one-third at a time until fully incorporated.

4 Using a 3-tablespoon scoop, portion the dough onto the prepared baking sheets, spacing the cookies at least 2 inches apart. Freeze until firm, about 1 hour.

5 Preheat the oven to 350°F.

6 Bake one sheet at a time for about 14 minutes, until set. Remove from the oven and let cool completely, about 1 hour. Repeat with the remaining baking sheet. Store in an airtight container at room temperature for up to 3 days.

Cake Batter Macarons

Makes
24 macarons

My first cookbook, *Dana's Bakery*, had a whole chapter of cake batter–flavored goodies. The Cake Batter Truffle was so popular that we ended up using it as a filling for a limited run of cake batter macarons. We don't have them available year-round, so I knew I needed to share the recipe here. Microwaving the flour ensures any harmful bacteria is killed, making it safe to use for the edible cake batter macaron filling.

MACARON SHELLS

4 large egg whites, at room temperature

1 teaspoon egg white powder

Pinch of kosher salt

1 cup (200 grams) granulated sugar

1½ cups (145 grams) almond flour

1½ cups (170 grams) powdered sugar

2 tablespoons rainbow nonpareil sprinkles

FILLING

1 cup (140 grams) gluten-free 1:1 replacement flour blend

4 tablespoons (½ stick) unsalted butter, at room temperature

¼ cup (50 grams) granulated sugar

1 teaspoon pure vanilla extract

¼ cup (50 grams) unsweetened applesauce

½ teaspoon kosher salt

2 tablespoons rainbow nonpareil sprinkles

1 **Make the macaron shells:** Preheat the oven to 325°F. Line two baking sheets with parchment paper or silicone baking mats.

2 In the bowl of a stand mixer fitted with the whisk attachment, beat the egg whites, egg white powder, and salt on medium-high speed until medium peaks form, about 4 minutes. With the mixer running, gradually add the granulated sugar and beat until stiff, glossy peaks form, about 3 minutes more. Sift the almond flour and powdered sugar on top of the meringue, then fold them into the meringue until the mixture falls back into the bowl off of a spoon in one continuous drip with no stiffness.

3 Transfer the batter to a piping bag fitted with a large round tip. If you are using parchment paper, pipe a little bit of the batter under each corner of the paper to secure it to the baking sheet. Pipe 1½-inch rounds of batter onto the prepared baking sheets, spacing them 1 inch apart. Sprinkle with the nonpareils. Slam each baking sheet onto your work surface six to eight times to release any air bubbles. Let the macarons stand at room temperature until a skin forms on the surface of the batter, 15 to 30 minutes.

4 Bake for 15 minutes, rotating the pans from front to back halfway through, until the macaron shells are crisp and firm on the outside. Remove from the oven and let cool completely, about 1 hour.

5 **Meanwhile, make the filling:** Place the flour in a small microwave-safe bowl and microwave on high in 30-second intervals, stirring after each, for 2 minutes. Set aside to cool.

6 In the bowl of a stand mixer fitted with the paddle attachment or in a large bowl using a

handheld mixer, combine the butter, granulated sugar, and vanilla and beat on medium speed until light and fluffy, about 2 minutes. Beat in the applesauce until fully incorporated, about 30 seconds. Beat in the flour and salt until combined, about 30 seconds.

7 Pipe or spoon about 1 teaspoon of the filling onto the flat side of half the macaron shells. Sandwich the filling with the remaining macaron shells, flat-side down. Store in an airtight container in the refrigerator for up to 5 days or in the freezer for up to 3 months.

Oatmeal Raisin Cookies

Makes
16 cookies

I love a classic oatmeal raisin cookie, but my daughters will only eat them if I swap out the raisins for chocolate chips. We meet halfway—I stir the dried fruit into half the dough for myself and put chocolate chips in the other half for them.

- 2 cups (250 grams) gluten-free rolled oats
- 1½ cups (205 grams) gluten-free 1:1 replacement flour blend
- 1 teaspoon ground cinnamon
- 1 teaspoon baking powder
- ½ teaspoon kosher salt
- 1 cup (2 sticks) unsalted butter, at room temperature
- ½ cup (100 grams) granulated sugar
- ½ cup packed (105 grams) brown sugar
- 2 large eggs, at room temperature
- 1 teaspoon pure vanilla extract
- 1½ cups (200 grams) raisins or chocolate chips

1 Preheat the oven to 350°F. Line two baking sheets with parchment paper.

2 In a medium bowl, whisk together the oats, flour, cinnamon, baking powder, and salt.

3 In a large bowl, combine the butter, granulated sugar, and brown sugar and beat with a handheld mixer on medium-high speed until light and fluffy, about 2 minutes. Beat in the eggs and vanilla until smooth, about 30 seconds more. Fold the dry ingredients into the wet ingredients one-third at a time until fully incorporated. Fold in the raisins.

4 Using a 3-tablespoon scoop, portion the dough onto the prepared baking sheets, spacing the cookies at least 2 inches apart. Bake one sheet at a time for 15 minutes, until the edges are golden. Remove from the oven and let cool completely, about 1 hour. Repeat with the remaining baking sheet. Store in an airtight container at room temperature for up to 3 days.

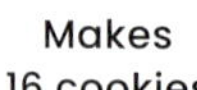

Crispy Chocolate Chip Cookies

Makes
16 cookies

There's just something about a perfectly executed thin chocolate chip cookie, and there's no reason the gluten-free community should miss out on that. I took inspiration from Sarah Kieffer's pan-banging cookies and used the technique on my go-to GF CCC recipe. The result is perfection.

- 2 cups (275 grams) gluten-free 1:1 replacement flour blend
- ½ teaspoon baking soda
- ½ teaspoon kosher salt
- 1 cup (2 sticks) unsalted butter, melted
- 1 cup (200 grams) granulated sugar
- ½ cup packed (105 grams) light brown sugar
- 1 large egg, at room temperature
- 1 teaspoon pure vanilla extract
- 1 (6-ounce) dark chocolate bar, chopped (about 2 cups)
- Flaky sea salt, for garnish (optional)

1 Preheat the oven to 350°F. Line two baking sheets with parchment paper.

2 In a medium bowl, whisk together the flour, baking soda, and salt.

3 In a large bowl, whisk together the melted butter, granulated sugar, and brown sugar until combined. Whisk in the egg and vanilla until smooth. Fold the dry ingredients into the wet ingredients one-third at a time until fully incorporated. Fold in the chopped chocolate.

4 Using a 3-tablespoon scoop, portion the dough onto the prepared baking sheets, spacing the cookies at least 2 inches apart. Sprinkle with flaky salt, if desired.

5 Bake one sheet at a time for 15 minutes, removing the pan from the oven every 5 minutes and banging it on the stovetop or another heatproof surface, then immediately returning it to the oven. Remove from the oven and let cool completely, about 1 hour. Repeat with the remaining baking sheet. Store in an airtight container at room temperature for up to 3 days.

Confetti Shortbread Cookies

Makes about 24 cookies

Nothing beats the simplicity of a classic crumbly shortbread cookie, but my girls love rainbow anything and insisted I give these a little move flair. Stirring the sprinkles into the dough adds a nice bit of crunch to the tender texture of the cookie—plus, they look so festive with barely any work. When I want to make these even more fun, I dip them in melted chocolate and decorate them with even more sprinkles.

- 1¼ cups (175 grams) gluten-free 1:1 replacement flour blend
- ½ cup (100 grams) sugar
- ½ teaspoon kosher salt
- ½ cup (1 stick) cold unsalted butter, cut into small cubes
- 1 large egg
- 1 teaspoon pure vanilla extract
- ¼ cup (35 grams) rainbow sprinkles

1 In the bowl of a stand mixer fitted with the paddle attachment, combine the flour, sugar, and salt and mix briefly on low speed to combine. Add the butter and beat on medium speed until the mixture has a coarse breadcrumb texture. Beat in the egg and vanilla until a smooth dough forms. Fold in the sprinkles.

2 Transfer the dough to a piece of plastic wrap and roll it into a 9-inch-long log, 1½ inches thick. Refrigerate until firm, at least 1 hour or up to 1 day.

3 Preheat the oven to 350°F. Line two baking sheets with parchment paper.

4 Unwrap the dough and cut the log crosswise into ¼-inch-thick slices. Place the dough rounds on the prepared baking sheets and prick each one with a fork. Bake one sheet at a time for about 15 minutes, until lightly golden on the edges. Remove from the oven and let cool completely before serving, about 15 minutes. Repeat with the remaining baking sheet.

5 Store in an airtight container at room temperature for up to 4 days.

BRING ON THE CHOCOLATE!

Make chocolate shortbread cookies by simply swapping out ¼ cup (35 grams) of the flour for ¼ cup (25 grams) unsweetened cocoa powder.

Cut-Out Sugar Cookies

Makes
24 cookies

I've always been a buttercream-on-sugar-cookies girl—my daughters love to slather the frosting on thick and cover them with sprinkles—but these are also great if you want to get fancy with some royal icing and a piping bag. Or make a simple icing with powdered sugar and lemon juice, then swirl some food coloring into it and dip each cookie into the icing for a tie-dye effect that couldn't be easier to pull off.

- 1½ cups (205 grams) gluten-free 1:1 replacement flour blend, plus more for dusting
- ¼ teaspoon baking powder
- ¼ teaspoon kosher salt
- ½ cup (1 stick) unsalted butter, at room temperature
- ½ cup (100 grams) sugar
- 1 large egg
- 1 teaspoon pure vanilla extract

1 Preheat the oven to 350°F. Line two baking sheets with parchment paper.

2 In a medium bowl, whisk together the flour, baking powder, and salt.

3 In the bowl of a stand mixer fitted with the paddle attachment, beat the butter and sugar on medium-high speed until light and fluffy, about 3 minutes. Beat in the egg until smooth. Beat in the vanilla. With the mixer on low, gradually beat in the dry ingredients until fully incorporated.

4 Divide the dough in half and place each portion on a piece of plastic wrap. Flatten each portion into a disc, wrap them tightly, and refrigerate until firm, about 1 hour.

5 Working with one dough disc at a time, on a lightly floured surface, roll out the dough to ¼-inch thickness, then use cookie cutters to cut out cookies and transfer them to the prepared baking sheets. Press the scraps together into a disc, wrap in plastic wrap, and return it to the fridge while you work on the other dough disc. Repeat until you've used up all the dough.

6 Bake one sheet at a time for 11 minutes, or until the bottoms are browned. Remove from the oven and let cool completely, about 30 minutes. Repeat with the remaining baking sheet.

7 Decorate the cooled cookies as desired. Store in an airtight container at room temperature for up to 4 days or in the freezer for up to 3 months.

Chocolate-Covered Strawberry Macarons

Makes
24 macarons

We developed this macaron for a Valentine's Day special at the bakery. It did so well that we added it to the menu, where it held the number one spot for years. It makes an appearance from time to time, but now you can have them all year round.

- 1 cup (20 grams) freeze-dried strawberries
- 4 large egg whites, at room temperature
- 1 teaspoon egg white powder
- Pinch of kosher salt
- 1 drop red or pink gel food coloring
- 1 cup (200 grams) granulated sugar
- 1 cup (95 grams) almond flour
- 1½ cups (170 grams) powdered sugar
- ½ cup (160 grams) seedless strawberry jam
- 2 cups (340 grams) semisweet chocolate chips
- 2 teaspoons coconut oil

1 Preheat the oven to 325°F. Line two baking sheets with parchment paper or silicone baking mats.

2 In a mini food processor, pulse the freeze-dried strawberries until you have a fine powder. Sift the powder to remove any large chunks.

3 In the bowl of a stand mixer fitted with the whisk attachment, beat the egg whites, egg white powder, salt, and food coloring on medium-high speed until medium peaks form, about 4 minutes. With the mixer running, gradually add the granulated sugar and beat until stiff, glossy peaks form, about 3 minutes more. Sift the almond flour, powdered sugar, and strawberry powder on top of the meringue, then fold them into the meringue until the mixture falls back into the bowl off of a spoon in one continuous drip with no stiffness.

4 Fit a piping bag with a large round tip and transfer the batter to the bag. If you are using parchment, pipe some batter under each corner of the paper to secure it. Pipe 1½-inch rounds of batter onto the prepared pans, 1 inch apart. Slam each baking sheet onto your work surface six to eight times to release any air bubbles. Let the macarons stand at room temperature until a skin forms on the surface of the batter, 15 to 30 minutes.

5 Bake for 15 minutes, rotating the pans from front to back halfway through, until the macaron shells are firm. Remove from the oven and let cool completely, about 1 hour.

6 Pipe or spoon about 1 teaspoon of the jam onto the flat side of half the macaron shells. Sandwich the filling with the remaining macaron shells, flat-side down.

7 Place the chocolate chips and coconut oil in a large glass measuring cup and microwave in 30-second intervals, stirring after each, until melted and smooth.

8 Set a wire rack over a piece of parchment paper. Dip half of each macaron in the melted chocolate, then transfer to the rack. Let stand until the chocolate is set, about 30 minutes. Store in an airtight container in the refrigerator for up to 5 days or in the freezer for up to 3 months.

CAKES

Red Velvet Cake

Makes one 8-inch two-layer cake; serves 12 to 14

To get the vibrant color that red velvet is known for, gel food coloring works best—it's thick and requires less to get rich color than liquid food dyes. You can use natural food dye if you prefer, but the color won't be as bright. I like to use the "naked" frosting method on this cake: Spread half the frosting between the layers and the other half on top so that beautiful color still shines through. Use leftover cake in the ice cream recipe on page 192.

CAKE

- Nonstick cooking spray
- 2½ cups (350 grams) gluten-free 1:1 replacement flour blend
- 3 tablespoons unsweetened cocoa powder
- 1 tablespoon baking powder
- 1 teaspoon kosher salt
- 6 tablespoons (¾ stick) unsalted butter, at room temperature
- 6 tablespoons (75 grams) neutral oil, such as avocado, sunflower, grapeseed, or canola oil
- 2 cups (400 grams) granulated sugar
- 4 large eggs
- 2 teaspoons pure vanilla extract
- 1 teaspoon distilled white or apple cider vinegar
- 30 drops red gel food coloring
- ⅔ cup (110 grams) buttermilk

FROSTING

- ½ cup (1 stick) unsalted butter, at room temperature
- 1 (8-ounce) block full-fat cream cheese, at room temperature
- 4 cups (455 grams) powdered sugar
- 1 tablespoon whole milk
- 1 teaspoon pure vanilla extract

1 **Make the cake:** Preheat the oven to 350°F. Line two 8-inch cake pans with parchment paper cut to fit and spray with cooking spray.

2 In a medium bowl, whisk together the flour, cocoa powder, baking powder, and salt.

3 In the bowl of a stand mixer fitted with the paddle attachment or in a large bowl using a handheld mixer, beat the butter, oil, and granulated sugar on medium speed until fluffy, about 2 minutes. Add the eggs one at a time, beating until smooth after each addition. Beat in the vanilla, vinegar, and food coloring. Add the dry ingredients in three additions, alternating with the buttermilk, and beat until smooth, about 30 seconds.

4 Divide the batter evenly between the prepared pans. Bake for about 40 minutes, until a toothpick inserted into the center of each cake comes out with just a few moist crumbs attached. Remove from the oven and let the cakes cool in the pans for at least 1 hour, then transfer to a wire rack to cool completely, at least 1 hour more.

5 **Make the frosting:** In the bowl of a stand mixer fitted with the whisk attachment or in a large bowl using a handheld mixer, beat the butter, cream cheese, powdered sugar, milk, and vanilla on medium speed until smooth. Scrape down the sides and beat on high until fluffy, 2 to 5 minutes.

6 Spread or pipe frosting on top of one cooled cake layer. Stack the second layer on top and then spread or pipe the remaining frosting over the top and sides of the cake. Refrigerate until ready to serve, up to 1 day.

Confetti Birthday Cake

Makes one 8-inch three-layer cake; serves 12 to 14

Rainbow sprinkles give this old-school birthday cake that classic look, but you can leave them out and still have a delicious vanilla layer cake. If you are opting for the pop of color, be sure to use rod-shaped sprinkles rather than round nonpareils or another shape for the best confetti-like color distribution.

CAKE

- Nonstick cooking spray
- 2¾ cups (380 grams) gluten-free 1:1 replacement flour blend
- 1 tablespoon baking powder
- 1 teaspoon kosher salt
- 6 tablespoons (¾ stick) unsalted butter, at room temperature
- 6 tablespoons (75 grams) neutral oil, such as avocado, sunflower, grapeseed, or canola oil
- 2 cups (400 grams) granulated sugar
- 4 large eggs
- 2 teaspoons pure vanilla extract
- ⅔ cup (150 grams) whole milk
- ½ cup (70 grams) rainbow sprinkles, plus more for decorating

FROSTING

- 1½ cups (3 sticks) unsalted butter, at room temperature
- 6 cups (680 grams) powdered sugar
- 3 tablespoons whole milk
- 2 teaspoons pure vanilla extract

1 **Make the cake:** Preheat the oven to 350°F. Line three 8-inch cake pans with parchment paper cut to fit the bottom of the pan and spray with cooking spray.

2 In a medium bowl, whisk together the flour, baking powder, and salt.

3 In the bowl of a stand mixer fitted with the paddle attachment or in a large bowl using a handheld mixer, combine the butter, oil, and granulated sugar and beat on medium speed until fluffy, about 2 minutes. Add the eggs one at a time, beating until smooth after each addition. Beat in the vanilla. Add the dry ingredients in three additions, alternating with the milk, and beat until smooth, about 1 minute. Fold in the sprinkles.

4 Divide the batter evenly among the prepared pans. Bake for 25 to 30 minutes, until a toothpick inserted into the center of each cake comes out with just a few moist crumbs attached. Remove from the oven and let the cakes cool in the pans for at least 1 hour, then transfer to a wire rack to cool completely, at least 1 hour more.

5 **Meanwhile, make the frosting:** In the bowl of a stand mixer fitted with the whisk attachment or in a large bowl using a handheld mixer, combine the butter, powdered sugar, milk, and vanilla and beat on medium speed until combined. Scrape down the sides of the bowl and beat on high until light and fluffy, 2 to 5 minutes.

6 Spread or pipe the frosting on top of one cooled cake layer. Stack the second layer on the first and spread or pipe more frosting over the top. Stack the final cake layer on top and spread or pipe the remaining frosting over the top and sides of the cake. Decorate with more sprinkles.

Strawberries & Cream Cake

Makes one 8-inch two-layer cake; serves 12 to 14

This cake was inspired by my grandma Doris. I created this nod to her favorite dessert by replacing the shortcakes with fluffy white cake layers covered in whipped cream and strawberries. I love the presentation of this cake at a party, and it's way easier than serving up individual shortcakes.

CAKE

- Nonstick cooking spray
- 3 cups (415 grams) gluten-free 1:1 replacement flour blend
- 1 tablespoon baking powder
- 1 teaspoon kosher salt
- 6 tablespoons (¾ stick) unsalted butter, at room temperature
- 6 tablespoons (75 grams) neutral oil, such as avocado, sunflower, grapeseed, or canola oil
- 2 cups (400 grams) granulated sugar
- 6 large egg whites
- 2 teaspoons pure vanilla extract
- 1 cup (225 grams) whole milk

FILLING

- 1 pound fresh strawberries, sliced
- 1 tablespoon granulated sugar
- 2 cups (455 grams) heavy cream
- 2 tablespoons powdered sugar
- 1 teaspoon pure vanilla extract

1 **Make the cake:** Preheat the oven to 350°F. Line two 8-inch cake pans with parchment paper cut to fit the bottom of the pan and spray with cooking spray.

2 In a medium bowl, combine the flour, baking powder, and salt.

3 In the bowl of a stand mixer fitted with the paddle attachment or in a large bowl using a handheld mixer, combine the butter, oil, and granulated sugar and beat on medium speed until fluffy, about 2 minutes. Add the egg whites one at a time, beating until smooth after each addition. Beat in the vanilla. Add the dry ingredients in three additions, alternating with the milk, and beat until smooth.

4 Divide the batter evenly between the prepared pans. Bake for about 40 minutes, until a toothpick inserted into the center of each cake comes out with just a few moist crumbs attached. Remove from the oven and let cool in the pans for about 1 hour, then transfer to a wire rack to cool completely, about 1 hour.

5 **Make the filling:** In a medium bowl, toss the strawberries with the granulated sugar.

6 In the bowl of a stand mixer fitted with the whisk attachment or in a large bowl using a handheld mixer, combine the cream, powdered sugar, and vanilla and beat on medium-high speed until medium peaks form, 2 to 5 minutes.

7 Top one cooled cake layer with half the macerated strawberries, then half the cream. Top with the second cake layer and pile the remaining cream and strawberries on top. Serve immediately.

Flourless Peanut Butter–Chocolate Mug Cake

Makes
1 mug cake

I always need a sweet treat to end my day, but I don't always have the energy to whip up a whole dessert. That's when mug cake comes to the rescue! This decadent version has its roots in flourless chocolate cake with a peanut butter twist, and it comes together in your microwave in just minutes.

- 2 tablespoons unsalted butter
- ¼ cup (45 grams) semisweet chocolate chips
- 1 large egg
- 1 tablespoon unsweetened cocoa powder
- 1 tablespoon granulated sugar
- ½ teaspoon pure vanilla extract
- Pinch of kosher salt
- 1 tablespoon creamy peanut butter
- Powdered sugar, for dusting (optional)

1 Place the butter and chocolate chips in a microwave-safe mug or ramekin and microwave in 30-second intervals, stirring after each, until melted and smooth. Whisk in the egg, cocoa powder, granulated sugar, vanilla, and salt. Dollop the peanut butter on top and use a butter knife to swirl it into the batter.

2 Microwave for about 2½ minutes, until the top is set. Let cool for at least 5 minutes before serving. Dust with powdered sugar, if desired, and enjoy.

Tiramisu Trifle

Makes
1 trifle dish;
serves about 12

The first time I made this tiramisu, my husband and I ate half of it in one sitting, so I decided to double the recipe for this book! I love the presentation a trifle dish gives classic tiramisu—plus, it makes the tiramisu easier to serve. Just scoop up mounds and serve in bowl; no need to carefully lift out perfectly square slices. Or do as Adam and I did and just dive right into the dish with a spoon.

LADYFINGERS

- 6 large eggs, separated
- 1 cup (200 grams) granulated sugar
- 2 cups (275 grams) gluten-free 1:1 replacement flour blend
- ¼ cup (30 grams) cornstarch
- Pinch of kosher salt
- ¼ cup (30 grams) powdered sugar

TIRAMISU

- 8 large egg yolks
- 1 cup (200 grams) granulated sugar
- 2 cups (455 grams) heavy cream
- 2 (8-ounce) containers mascarpone
- 2 teaspoons pure vanilla extract
- Pinch of kosher salt
- 5 tablespoons (30 grams) unsweetened cocoa powder
- 1 cup (225 grams) brewed coffee, cooled
- 2 tablespoons rum

1 **Make the ladyfingers:** Preheat the oven to 350°F. Line two baking sheets with parchment paper.

2 In a medium bowl, beat the egg yolks and ½ cup (100 grams) of the granulated sugar with a handheld mixer on medium-high speed until pale and fluffy, about 1 minute. Wipe the beaters clean.

3 In a large bowl using the handheld mixer, beat the egg whites on medium-high until foamy, about 1 minute. With the mixer running on medium-high, gradually add the remaining ½ cup (100 grams) granulated sugar and beat until stiff peaks form, about 4 minutes.

4 Fold the egg yolk mixture into the egg white mixture. Sift the flour, cornstarch, and salt over the egg mixture and gently fold in the dry ingredients until completely combined, about 30 seconds. Transfer the batter to a large zip-top bag and snip one corner off, creating a ½-inch hole. Pipe the batter onto the prepared baking sheets in 3×1-inch ovals. Dust the batter with the powdered sugar.

5 Bake one sheet at a time for about 15 minutes, until lightly golden and set. Remove from the oven and let cool completely, about 1 hour. Repeat with the remaining baking sheet.

6 **Make the tiramisu:** In a medium bowl, beat the egg yolks and ½ cup (100 grams) of the granulated sugar with a handheld mixer on medium speed until pale and fluffy, about 1 minute. Wipe the beaters clean.

7 In a large bowl using the handheld mixer, beat the cream and remaining ½ cup (100 grams) granulated sugar on medium-high until soft peaks form, about 3 minutes. Add the

Recipe continues

mascarpone, vanilla, and salt and beat until medium peaks form, about 1 minute. Fold the egg yolk mixture into the mascarpone mixture.

8 Sprinkle the bottom of a trifle dish with 1 tablespoon of the cocoa powder. In a shallow dish, stir together the coffee and rum. Dip one-quarter of the ladyfingers in the coffee mixture one at a time, flipping to coat both sides, then arrange them over the bottom of the trifle dish on top of the cocoa powder. Top the layer of ladyfingers with one-quarter of the mascarpone mixture. Sprinkle 1 tablespoon of the cocoa powder over the mascarpone. Repeat with the remaining ladyfingers, coffee mixture, mascarpone, and cocoa powder to create four total layers.

9 Cover and refrigerate for at least 4 hours or up to 2 days before serving.

Carrot Cake

Makes one 8-inch two-layer cake; serves 12 to 14

Carrots are always the stars of my garden. My kids love to dig them up, and what better way to use them than in this gluten-free version of classic carrot cake, which bakes up nice and moist thanks to full-fat Greek yogurt. Give the cake some flair by decorating with the candied carrots shown here, or use edible flowers (I grow these every year, too!). Just make sure you wait until serving to put them on so they don't get too wilted while sitting out.

CAKE

- Nonstick cooking spray
- 2½ cups (350 grams) gluten-free 1:1 replacement flour blend
- 1 tablespoon ground cinnamon
- 1 tablespoon baking powder
- 1 teaspoon kosher salt
- ¾ cup (1½ sticks) unsalted butter, at room temperature
- 2 cups packed (435 grams) light brown sugar
- 4 large eggs
- 1 cup (255 grams) plain full-fat Greek yogurt
- 2 teaspoons pure vanilla extract
- 1 pound carrots, shredded

CANDIED CARROTS

- 2 large carrots
- 2 cups granulated sugar

FROSTING

- ½ cup (1 stick) unsalted butter, at room temperature
- 1 (8-ounce) block full-fat cream cheese, at room temperature
- 4 cups (455 grams) powdered sugar
- 1 tablespoon whole milk
- 1 teaspoon pure vanilla extract

1 **Make the cake:** Preheat the oven to 350°F. Line two 8-inch cake pans with parchment paper cut to fit the bottom of the pan and spray with cooking spray.

2 In a medium bowl, whisk together the flour, cinnamon, baking powder, and salt.

3 In the bowl of a stand mixer fitted with the paddle attachment or in a large bowl using a handheld mixer, beat the butter and brown sugar on medium speed until fluffy, about 2 minutes. Add the eggs one at a time, beating until smooth after each addition. Beat in the yogurt and vanilla until smooth. Add the dry ingredients and beat until smooth. Fold in the carrots.

4 Divide the batter evenly between the prepared pans. Bake for about 40 minutes, until a toothpick inserted into the center of each cake comes out with just a few moist crumbs attached.

5 Remove from the oven and let the cakes cool in the pans for about 1 hour, then transfer to a wire rack to cool completely, about 1 hour more.

6 **Meanwhile, make the candied carrots:** Run a vegetable peeler lengthwise down the carrots to slice them into long, thin ribbons.

7 In a large saucepan, stir together the granulated sugar and 1 cup water. Cook over medium-high heat, stirring, until the sugar has

Recipe continues

dissolved and the mixture comes to a boil. Add the carrot ribbons and cook, stirring, for 5 minutes. Drain and set on a piece of parchment paper to cool.

8 **Meanwhile, make the frosting:** In the bowl of a stand mixer fitted with the whisk attachment or in a large bowl using a handheld mixer, combine the butter, cream cheese, powdered sugar, milk, and vanilla and beat on medium speed until combined. Scrape down the sides of the bowl and beat on high until light and fluffy, 2 to 5 minutes.

9 Spread or pipe frosting on top of one cooled cake layer. Stack the second layer on top and then spread or pipe the remaining frosting over the top and sides of the cake. Top the cake with the candied carrots. Refrigerate until ready to serve, up to 1 day.

Upside-Down Bananas Foster Cake

Makes one 9-inch cake; serves 8 to 12

The caramelized banana topping on this rum-infused cake gets flambéed before serving for the full bananas Foster experience. Just be sure to use a rum that's at least 80 proof, or it won't light. I like to use spiced rum for added flavor.

Nonstick cooking spray

TOPPING

4 tablespoons (½ stick) unsalted butter, melted

¼ cup packed (55 grams) dark brown sugar

1 teaspoon pure vanilla extract

½ teaspoon ground cinnamon

3 large bananas (540 grams), peeled

CAKE

1½ cups (205 grams) gluten-free 1:1 replacement flour blend

1 teaspoon baking powder

½ teaspoon kosher salt

3 tablespoons unsalted butter, at room temperature

3 tablespoons neutral oil, such as avocado, sunflower, grapeseed, or canola oil

½ cup (100 grams) granulated sugar

2 large eggs

2 tablespoons 100-proof rum, plus more for drizzling

1 teaspoon pure vanilla extract

1 Preheat the oven to 350°F. Line an 8-inch springform pan with aluminum foil and coat it with cooking spray. Wrap the outside of the pan in more foil to prevent any leaks.

2 **Make the topping:** In a small bowl, whisk together the melted butter, brown sugar, vanilla, and cinnamon. Pour the mixture into the bottom of the prepared pan. Cut the bananas in half crosswise and then halve them again lengthwise. Place the banana quarters flat-side down in the pan on top of the sauce.

3 **Make the cake:** In a medium bowl, whisk together the flour, baking powder, and salt.

4 In the bowl of a stand mixer fitted with the paddle attachment or in a large bowl using a handheld mixer, combine the butter, oil, and granulated sugar and beat on medium-high speed until light and fluffy, about 2 minutes. Beat in the eggs one at a time until smooth. Beat in the rum and vanilla. Add the dry ingredients and beat until smooth, about 30 seconds.

5 Spread the batter over the bananas in the pan. Bake for about 45 minutes, until the cake is golden and a toothpick inserted into the center comes out with just a few moist crumbs attached. Remove from the oven and let cool for 30 minutes, then invert the cake onto a plate and peel off the foil.

6 Just before serving, drizzle the cake with the rum and use a long lighter to ignite the alcohol, flambéing the cake. Serve immediately.

Dirt Cup Poke Cake

Makes one 9 × 13-inch cake; serves 18 to 24

To be honest, I prefer this cake without the Oreo crumbs and gummy worms, but certain members of my family are wild for them (hi, Ella!). So when my kids aren't involved, I skip them and decorate this chocolate poke cake with chocolate shavings by running a vegetable peeler over a bar of dark chocolate.

CAKE

- Nonstick cooking spray
- 1¾ cups (240 grams) gluten-free 1:1 replacement flour blend
- ¾ cup (75 grams) unsweetened cocoa powder
- 1½ teaspoons baking powder
- 1½ teaspoons baking soda
- 1 teaspoon kosher salt
- 2 cups (400 grams) sugar
- ½ cup (100 grams) neutral oil, such as avocado, sunflower, grapeseed, or canola oil
- 2 large eggs
- 2 teaspoons pure vanilla extract
- 1 cup (225 grams) whole milk
- 1 cup (240 grams) hot water

TOPPING

- 1 (5-ounce) package instant chocolate pudding mix
- 3 cups (680 grams) cold whole milk
- 2 cups (455 grams) heavy cream
- 15 gluten-free chocolate sandwich cookies, such as gluten-free Oreos (170 grams)
- Gummy worms, for garnish

1 **Make the cake:** Preheat the oven to 350°F. Coat a 9 × 13-inch baking pan with cooking spray.

2 In a medium bowl, combine the flour, cocoa powder, baking powder, baking soda, and salt.

3 In the bowl of a stand mixer fitted with the paddle attachment or in a large bowl using a handheld mixer, combine the sugar, oil, eggs, and vanilla and beat on medium speed until combined, about 30 seconds. Add the dry ingredients in three additions, alternating with the milk, and beat until smooth. Add the hot water and beat until combined and smooth (the batter will be very thin), about 30 seconds.

4 Pour the batter into the prepared pan. Bake for about 45 minutes, until a toothpick inserted into the center comes out with just a few moist crumbs attached. Remove the pan from the oven and use the handle of a wooden spoon to poke holes three-quarters of the way into the depth of the cake, spacing the holes 1 inch apart.

5 **Make the topping:** In a large glass measuring cup or large bowl, whisk together the pudding mix and the cold milk until the mix has dissolved. Immediately pour 2 cups of the mixture over the cake and refrigerate until cool, about 2 hours. Let the remaining pudding mixture set at room temperature until thick, about 5 minutes.

6 Meanwhile, in a large bowl using a handheld mixer, beat the cream on medium speed until soft peaks form, about 2 minutes. Fold in the thickened pudding mixture.

7 In a food processor, pulse the cookies until fine crumbs form.

8 Spread the whipped cream over the chilled cake. Sprinkle the cookie crumbs, then scatter the gummy worms on top. Refrigerate until ready to serve, up to 1 day.

Raspberry Swirl Cheesecake

Makes one 9-inch cheesecake; serves 12 to 16

My girls love the pink swirl that raspberries give this cheesecake, but you could swap in any other berry. Letting the cheesecake cool slowly in the oven with the door cracked after baking prevents the top from cracking.

- Nonstick cooking spray
- 1 (6-ounce) container fresh raspberries
- 1¼ cups (250 grams) sugar
- 2 tablespoons fresh lemon juice
- 1 (6- to 7-ounce) box gluten-free graham crackers (12 graham crackers/210 grams)
- 4 tablespoons (½ stick) unsalted butter, melted
- 3 (8-ounce) blocks full-fat cream cheese, at room temperature
- 3 large eggs
- ¾ cup (170 grams) heavy cream
- 3 tablespoons gluten-free 1:1 replacement flour blend
- 1 teaspoon pure vanilla extract
- ½ teaspoon kosher salt

1 Preheat the oven to 325°F. Wrap the outside of a 9-inch springform pan in aluminum foil so the bottom and sides are completely covered. Lightly spray the inside of the pan with cooking spray.

2 In a small saucepan, combine the raspberries, ¼ cup of the sugar, and 1 tablespoon of the lemon juice. Bring to a boil over medium-high heat, then reduce the heat to a simmer and cook, stirring occasionally, until thickened, about 5 minutes. Carefully transfer the mixture to a blender and puree until smooth. Pour the mixture through a fine-mesh sieve set over a small bowl, pressing on the solids with a rubber spatula to release as much liquid as possible; discard the solids.

3 Pulse the graham crackers in a food processor until finely ground. With the motor running, drizzle in the melted butter and process until the graham cracker crumbs start to clump together. Press the mixture into an even layer over the bottom of the prepared pan.

4 Wipe out the food processor, then add the cream cheese, eggs, cream, flour, vanilla, and salt. Add the remaining 1 cup sugar and 1 tablespoon lemon juice. Process until combined and smooth.

5 Transfer ½ cup of the cream cheese mixture to the bowl with the raspberry liquid and stir to combine. Pour half the cream cheese mixture on top of the graham cracker crust in the pan, then dollop in half the raspberry mixture. Use a butter knife to swirl the two mixtures together, being careful not to overmix. Repeat to make another layer with the remaining mixtures.

6 Set the springform pan in a large baking pan or roasting dish and fill the dish with hot water to come halfway up the sides of the springform pan. Bake for about 1 hour, until the cheesecake is set on top but still jiggly in the center. Turn the oven off, but leave the cake in the oven with the door cracked open until completely cooled, at least 2 hours. Refrigerate until chilled before serving, about 8 hours, or for up to 2 days.

Neapolitan Bundt Cake

Makes 1 Bundt cake; serves 12 to 16

The key to getting vibrant, colorful strawberry, chocolate, and vanilla layers on the outside of this cake is baking it in a silicone Bundt pan. The silicone prevents the browning you'd get from a metal pan so that the pink and white layers really pop. You can order one online, and it's so worth it! The freeze-dried strawberry powder adds great flavor, but only a touch of pink color, so to get really distinct layers, I add a bit of red gel food dye (see the headnote on page 51) to the strawberry batter.

CAKE

- Nonstick cooking spray
- 1 cup (20 grams) freeze-dried strawberries
- 2¼ cups (300 grams) gluten-free 1:1 replacement flour blend
- 1 tablespoon baking powder
- 1 teaspoon kosher salt
- 6 tablespoons (¾ stick) unsalted butter, at room temperature
- 6 tablespoons (75 grams) neutral oil, such as avocado, sunflower, grapeseed, or canola oil
- 2 cups (400 grams) sugar
- 4 large eggs
- 2 teaspoons pure vanilla extract
- ⅔ cup (150 grams) whole milk
- 1 drop red gel food coloring
- ¼ cup (25 grams) unsweetened cocoa powder

GANACHE

- ½ cup (85 grams) chocolate chips
- ⅓ cup (75 grams) heavy cream

- Sprinkles, for garnish

1 **Make the cake:** Preheat the oven to 350°F. Coat a silicone Bundt pan with cooking spray.

2 In a mini food processor, pulse the freeze-dried strawberries until you have a fine powder. Sift the powder to remove any large chunks.

3 In a medium bowl, combine 2 cups (265 grams) of the flour, the baking powder, and the salt.

4 In the bowl of a stand mixer fitted with the paddle attachment or in a large bowl using a handheld mixer, combine the butter, oil, and sugar and beat on medium speed until fluffy, about 2 minutes. Add the eggs one at a time, beating until smooth after each addition. Beat in the vanilla. Add the dry ingredients in three additions, alternating with the milk, and beat until smooth, about 30 seconds.

5 Divide the batter evenly among three medium bowls. Stir the remaining ¼ cup (35 grams) flour into the batter in the first bowl. Stir the strawberry powder and red food coloring into the batter in the second bowl, and stir the cocoa powder into the batter in the third bowl.

6 Pour the vanilla batter into the prepared pan, followed by the strawberry batter, and finally pour the chocolate batter on top. Bake for about 40 minutes, until a toothpick inserted into the center comes out with just a few moist crumbs attached. Remove from the oven and let the cake cool in the pan for at least 1 hour, then transfer to a wire rack to cool completely, at least 1 hour more.

7 **Make the ganache:** Place the chocolate chips in a small heatproof bowl or a large glass measuring cup. In a small saucepan, heat the cream over medium-high heat just until it comes to a boil. Pour the hot cream over the chocolate chips in the bowl and let stand for 1 minute, then whisk until smooth.

8 Pour the ganache over the cooled cake and decorate with sprinkles. Refrigerate until the ganache sets before serving, about 30 minutes, or for up to 1 day.

Chocolate Layer Cake

Makes one 8-inch two-layer cake; serves 12 to 14

Using coffee in this cake batter really enhances the rich flavor of the chocolate, but if you aren't a coffee drinker, don't fret. Hot water will work, too! This batter is super loose, but it will bake up perfectly into—dare I say—the most moist chocolate cake you've ever had.

CAKE

- Nonstick cooking spray
- 1¾ cups (240 grams) gluten-free 1:1 replacement flour blend
- ¾ cup (75 grams) unsweetened cocoa powder
- 1½ teaspoons baking powder
- 1½ teaspoons baking soda
- 1 teaspoon kosher salt
- 2 cups (400 grams) granulated sugar
- ½ cup (100 grams) neutral oil, such as avocado, sunflower, grapeseed, or canola oil
- 2 large eggs
- 2 teaspoons pure vanilla extract
- 1 cup (225 grams) whole milk
- 1 cup (225 grams) hot coffee

FROSTING

- ½ cup (1 stick) unsalted butter, melted
- 3 cups (340 grams) powdered sugar
- ⅔ cup (65 grams) unsweetened cocoa powder
- ⅓ cup (75 grams) whole milk
- 1 teaspoon pure vanilla extract

1 **Make the cake:** Preheat the oven to 350°F. Line two 8-inch cake pans with parchment paper cut to fit the bottom of the pan and spray with cooking spray.

2 In a medium bowl, combine the flour, cocoa powder, baking powder, baking soda, and salt.

3 In the bowl of a stand mixer fitted with the paddle attachment or in a large bowl using a handheld mixer, combine the granulated sugar, oil, eggs, and vanilla and beat on medium speed until combined. Add the dry ingredients in three additions, alternating with the milk, and beat until smooth. Add the hot coffee and beat until combined and smooth (the batter will be very thin).

4 Divide the batter evenly between the prepared pans. Bake for about 45 minutes, until a toothpick inserted into the center of each cake comes out with just a few moist crumbs attached. Remove from the oven and let the cakes cool in the pans for at least 1 hour, then transfer to a wire rack to cool completely, at least 1 hour more.

5 **Meanwhile, make the frosting:** In the bowl of a stand mixer fitted with the whisk attachment or in a large bowl using a handheld mixer, combine the melted butter, powdered sugar, cocoa powder, milk, and vanilla and beat on medium speed until combined. Scrape down the sides of the bowl and beat on high until light and fluffy, 2 to 5 minutes.

6 Spread or pipe the frosting on top of one cooled cake layer. Stack the second layer on top and then spread or pipe the remaining frosting over the top and sides of the cake. Refrigerate until ready to serve, up to 1 day.

BREADS

Chocolate Swirl Pumpkin Bread

Makes one 9 × 5-inch loaf; serves 8 to 10

Thanks to a full can of pumpkin puree, this pumpkin loaf has a moist, tender texture that's almost cakelike. Plus, the melted chocolate stirred into the batter for the chocolate swirl gives it a rich, brownie-like flavor.

- Nonstick cooking spray
- 2 cups (275 grams) gluten-free 1:1 replacement flour blend
- 1½ teaspoons baking powder
- 1 teaspoon ground cinnamon
- ½ teaspoon baking soda
- ½ teaspoon kosher salt
- 4 tablespoons (½ stick) unsalted butter, at room temperature
- 1 cup (200 grams) sugar
- 2 large eggs
- 1 (15-ounce) can pure pumpkin puree
- 1 teaspoon pure vanilla extract
- ¼ cup (40 grams) buttermilk
- ½ cup (85 grams) bittersweet chocolate chips

1 Preheat the oven to 350°F. Coat a 9 × 5-inch loaf pan with cooking spray.

2 In a medium bowl, whisk together the flour, baking powder, cinnamon, baking soda, and salt.

3 In a large bowl, beat the butter and sugar with a handheld mixer on medium speed until light and fluffy, about 2 minutes. Add the eggs one at a time and beat until fully incorporated. Beat in the pumpkin and vanilla. Add the dry ingredients, alternating with the buttermilk, and beat until fully combined.

4 In a small microwave-safe bowl, microwave the chocolate chips in 30-second intervals, stirring after each, until melted and smooth.

5 Transfer one-third of the batter to the bowl with the the melted chocolate and stir until thoroughly mixed. Transfer half the remaining plain batter to the prepared pan. Drizzle half the chocolate batter on top and swirl it into the plain batter using a butter knife, being careful not to overmix. Repeat with the remaining plain batter, then the remaining chocolate batter. Run a butter knife down the center of the batter in the pan for the perfect crack while baking.

6 Bake for about 2 hours, until a toothpick inserted into the center comes out clean. Let cool in the pan for at least 30 minutes, then transfer to a wire rack to cool completely before slicing and serving. Store in an airtight container at room temperature for up to 3 days.

Soft Pretzels

Makes
8 pretzels

You know that alluring smell hanging in the air when you walk past a pretzel stand in a mall? Now you can finally re-create it in your own home. Brushing with melted butter after baking gives these that nostalgic mall-pretzel flavor. Make a large batch and stash some away in the fridge or freezer to enjoy later. These are of course great with just a sprinkling of coarse salt or seasoned salt, but you can also make them sweet by sprinkling them with cinnamon-sugar instead.

- 2 tablespoons ground psyllium husk (see page 11)
- 2¾ cups (380 grams) gluten-free 1:1 replacement flour blend, plus more for dusting
- 5 tablespoons packed (60 grams) light brown sugar
- 1 tablespoon instant yeast
- 1 tablespoon kosher salt
- 1⅔ cups (400 grams) warm water
- 4 tablespoons (½ stick) unsalted butter, melted
- ¼ cup (70 grams) baking soda
- Toppings, such as flaky sea salt and/or seasoned salt

1 In the bowl of a stand mixer fitted with the paddle attachment, combine the psyllium husk, flour, 3 tablespoons of the brown sugar, the yeast, and the salt. Add the warm water and 2 tablespoons of the melted butter and beat on medium speed until combined. Scrape down the sides of the bowl and beat on medium-high until a stretchy dough forms. Scrape down the sides of the bowl so the dough is in a ball at the bottom. Cover with a clean kitchen towel and let rise until visibly risen and puffy, about 1 hour.

2 Preheat the oven to 425°F. Line two baking sheets with parchment paper. Bring a large pot of water to a boil over high heat.

3 Turn the dough out onto a floured surface, cut it into 8 equal pieces, and form each into a ball. Knead each dough ball until smooth, then, working with one at a time, roll each ball into a 20-inch-long rope. Place the rope in a U-shape on your work surface. Cross the ends over each other, twisting them once, then set them over the bottom of the U to form a pretzel shape. Repeat with the remaining dough balls.

4 Add the baking soda and the remaining 2 tablespoons brown sugar to the boiling water. Drop the pretzels into the water one at a time and boil until they float, about 5 seconds. Using a slotted spatula, transfer the pretzels to the prepared baking sheets, shaking off any excess water. Sprinkle the pretzels with your desired toppings.

5 Bake for 20 to 25 minutes, until golden. Remove from the oven and brush the tops with the remaining 2 tablespoons melted butter. Let cool slightly before eating.

6 Store leftover pretzels in an airtight container at room temperature for up to 3 days or in the freezer for up to 3 months. Reheat in the oven at 350°F for 10 minutes or in the toaster on the darkest setting before serving.

Chocolate Babka

Makes
1 loaf; serves 8 to 12

When I set out to write this book, I knew it needed to include a babka recipe—my all time favorite edible gift to hand out around the holidays. I'm a sucker for a gooey chocolate filling, but you could also do a cinnamon version by borrowing the filling recipe from the cinnamon buns on page 83.

DOUGH

1¾ cups (400 grams) whole milk, warmed

1 (¼-ounce) packet active dry yeast (2¼ teaspoons)

2 tablespoons unsalted butter, melted

1 large egg

1 teaspoon pure vanilla extract

3¼ cups (450 grams) gluten-free 1:1 replacement flour blend, plus more for dusting

2 tablespoons ground psyllium husk (see page 11)

¼ cup (50 grams) sugar

1½ teaspoons kosher salt

Nonstick cooking spray

FILLING

½ cup (85 grams) bittersweet chocolate chips

4 tablespoons (½ stick) unsalted butter

¼ cup (25 grams) unsweetened cocoa powder

¼ cup (50 grams) sugar

Pinch of kosher salt

1 large egg, lightly beaten, for egg wash

1 **Make the dough:** In a medium bowl or large glass measuring cup, whisk together the milk and yeast. Let stand for 5 minutes, until foamy. Add the melted butter, egg, and vanilla and whisk until combined.

2 In the bowl of a stand mixer fitted with the paddle attachment, combine the flour, psyllium husk, sugar, and salt. With the mixer running on low speed, slowly pour in the milk mixture. Increase the speed to medium-low and beat until a smooth dough forms. Shape the dough into a ball at the bottom of the bowl, cover, and let stand until visibly risen and puffy, 1 to 1½ hours.

3 Coat a 9 × 5-inch loaf pan with cooking spray. Lightly dust a baking sheet with flour.

4 **Make the filling:** Place the chocolate chips and butter in a medium microwave-safe bowl and microwave in 30-second intervals, whisking after each, until melted and smooth. Whisk in the cocoa powder, sugar, and salt.

5 On a lightly floured surface, roll the dough out to a 10 × 18-inch rectangle. Spread the filling evenly over the dough. Starting at one long end, roll the dough up into a log and transfer the log to the floured baking sheet. Refrigerate until firm, about 20 minutes.

6 Using a sharp knife, cut the log in half lengthwise, leaving 1 inch intact at the top. Twist the two strands up to reveal their cut sides, then twist the strands together. Pinch the ends of the strands together to seal, then tuck them under. Squish the two ends of the loaf toward each other to shorten up the babka, then transfer it

Recipe continues

to the prepared loaf pan. Cover and let rise until doubled in size, about 1 hour at room temperature or overnight in the fridge.

7 When ready to bake, preheat the oven 350°F.

8 Brush the bread with the egg wash. Bake the bread for about 45 minutes, until golden brown. Remove from the oven and let cool completely before removing the babka from the pan and slicing.

9 This babka is best served the day it's made, but you can store it in an airtight container at room temperature for up to 3 days. Toast before serving, or use the babka to make the French toast on page 87.

Cinnamon Morning Buns

Makes 12 buns

Soft and gooey cinnamon rolls just like you remember them—but finally gluten-free! The key to getting the perfect fluffy texture on these buns is pouring heavy cream over the rolls before the final rise and bake. The cream adds just enough moisture to the dough and also creates an extra-gooey sauce in the bottom of the pan that's perfect for drizzling on top of the buns before serving.

DOUGH

- 1¾ cups (400 grams) whole milk, warmed
- 1 (¼-ounce) packet active dry yeast (2¼ teaspoons)
- 2 tablespoons unsalted butter, melted
- 1 large egg
- 1 teaspoon pure vanilla extract
- 3¼ cups (450 grams) gluten-free 1:1 replacement flour blend, plus more for dusting
- 2 tablespoons ground psyllium husk (see page 11)
- ¼ cup (50 grams) granulated sugar
- 1½ teaspoons kosher salt

FILLING

- ¾ cup packed (160 grams) dark brown sugar
- 6 tablespoons (¾ stick) unsalted butter, melted
- 1½ tablespoons ground cinnamon
- Pinch of kosher salt
- Nonstick cooking spray
- ½ cup (115 grams) heavy cream

ICING

- 4 ounces full-fat cream cheese, at room temperature
- 1 cup (115 grams) powdered sugar
- 2 tablespoons heavy cream
- 1 teaspoon pure vanilla extract

1 Make the dough: In a medium bowl or large glass measuring cup, whisk together the milk and yeast. Let stand for 5 minutes, until foamy. Add the melted butter, egg, and vanilla to the milk mixture and whisk until combined.

2 In the bowl of a stand mixer fitted with the paddle attachment, combine the flour, psyllium husk, granulated sugar, and salt. With the mixer running on low speed, slowly pour in the milk mixture. Increase the speed to medium-low and beat until a smooth dough forms. Shape the dough into a ball at the bottom of the bowl, cover, and let stand until visibly risen and puffy, 1 to 1½ hours.

3 Make the filling: In a medium bowl, whisk together the brown sugar, melted butter, cinnamon, and salt.

4 Coat a 9×13-inch baking pan with cooking spray. On a lightly floured surface, roll the dough out to a 10×18-inch rectangle. Spread the filling evenly over the dough. Using a pizza cutter and starting at one long end, cut the dough into twelve 1½-inch-wide strips. Roll each strip up into a tight roll and place in the prepared pan. Pour the cream over the rolls in the pan. Cover and let rise until doubled in size, about 1 hour at room temperature or overnight in the fridge.

Recipe continues

5 When ready to bake, preheat the oven to 350°F.

6 Bake the rolls for about 30 minutes, until golden brown on top. Remove from the oven and let cool slightly, 5 to 10 minutes.

7 **Meanwhile, make the icing:** In a large bowl, combine the cream cheese, powdered sugar, cream, and vanilla and beat with a handheld mixer on medium speed until smooth, about 2 minutes.

8 Spread the icing over the warm rolls before serving. Store leftover rolls in an airtight container in the refrigerator for up to 3 days. Microwave for 30 seconds to rewarm before serving.

Babka French Toast

Makes 4 slices; serves 2 to 4

My babka recipe is really best eaten the same day it's made, but I not so secretly love when there is still some hanging around the next day so I can turn it into French toast. The bread gets a little crisp on the outside with a super-tender center that's oozing with melted chocolate. It's breakfast perfection.

2 large eggs

2 tablespoons whole milk

1 teaspoon ground cinnamon

1 teaspoon pure vanilla extract

1 tablespoon unsalted butter

4 (½-inch-thick) slices Chocolate Babka (page 81)

Maple syrup, chocolate syrup, and/or whipped cream, for serving

1 In a shallow bowl, whisk together the eggs, milk, cinnamon, and vanilla.

2 In a large nonstick skillet, melt ½ tablespoon of the butter over medium heat. Place two slices of the babka in the egg mixture and soak for 30 seconds, then flip and soak for 30 seconds more. Transfer to the pan and cook until golden on the bottom, 2 to 3 minutes. Flip and cook until golden on the other side, 2 to 3 minutes more. Transfer the French toast to a plate and repeat with the remaining babka and egg mixture.

3 Serve immediately, topped with maple syrup, chocolate syrup, and/or whipped cream.

Challah Bread Pudding

Makes
one 3-quart bread
pudding;
serves 12 to 16

Leftover challah—what's that? Though it's hard for me to imagine, I know there are times when you might not finish a whole loaf. If you end up with some challah lingering past its prime, this is the best way to put it to use. The thick, fluffy challah is perfect for soaking up the custard, making a creamy bread pudding. Don't feel like making your own crème anglaise? Just melt a pint of ice cream to drizzle on top—I promise it will be delicious either way.

BREAD PUDDING

Butter, for greasing

1 loaf Challah (page 96), cut into large cubes

2 large eggs

4 large egg yolks

2 cups (455 grams) heavy cream

1 cup (225 grams) whole milk

¾ cup (150 grams) sugar

1 tablespoon vanilla bean paste

CRÈME ANGLAISE

3 large egg yolks

¼ cup (50 grams) sugar

1 teaspoon vanilla bean paste

½ cup (115 grams) heavy cream

½ cup (115 grams) whole milk

1 **Make the bread pudding:** Preheat the oven to 350°F. Grease a 3-quart or larger baking dish with butter.

2 Place the challah cubes in the prepared baking dish.

3 In a large bowl, whisk together the eggs, egg yolks, cream, milk, sugar, and vanilla. Pour the egg mixture over the challah and press the cubes down to make sure they all get soaked with the egg mixture. Cover with aluminum foil and bake for about 45 minutes, until the center is almost set. Uncover and bake for about 30 minutes more, until the top is golden.

4 **Meanwhile, make the crème anglaise:** In a medium heatproof bowl, whisk together the egg yolks, sugar, and vanilla.

5 In a medium saucepan, whisk together the cream and milk. Bring to a boil over medium-high heat, then remove from the heat. While whisking continuously, slowly pour the hot cream mixture into the egg yolk mixture and whisk until combined. Return the mixture to the saucepan and cook over medium heat until thick enough to coat the back of a spoon, about 2 minutes.

6 Drizzle the crème anglaise over the pudding and serve immediately.

Zucchini Bread

Makes one 9 × 5-inch loaf; serves 8 to 10

There comes a time every year when my garden is absolutely bursting with zucchini, and this is the recipe Leni and Ella always ask me to make with it. They love helping me by grating the zucchini and stirring it into the batter, and I love anything that gets them excited about eating vegetables.

Nonstick cooking spray

2 cups (275 grams) gluten-free 1:1 replacement flour blend

1½ teaspoons baking powder

1 teaspoon ground cinnamon

½ teaspoon baking soda

½ teaspoon kosher salt

1 cup (200 grams) sugar

4 tablespoons (½ stick) unsalted butter, at room temperature

Zest of 1 lemon

2 large eggs

1 teaspoon pure vanilla extract

1 medium zucchini (1 pound), shredded (about 1½ cups)

¼ cup (40 grams) buttermilk

1 Preheat the oven to 350°F. Coat a 9 × 5-inch loaf pan with cooking spray.

2 In a medium bowl, whisk together the flour, baking powder, cinnamon, baking soda, and salt.

3 In the bowl of a stand mixer fitted with the paddle attachment or in a large bowl using a handheld mixer, combine the sugar, butter, and lemon zest and beat on medium speed until light and fluffy, 2 minutes. Add the eggs one at a time and beat until fully incorporated. Beat in the vanilla. Beat in the zucchini. Add the dry ingredients in three additions, alternating with the buttermilk, and beat until fully combined.

4 Transfer the batter to the prepared pan. Bake for about 1 hour, until a toothpick inserted into the center comes out clean. Let cool completely before slicing, about 1 hour.

5 Store in an airtight container at room temperature for up to 4 days.

Pull-Apart Cinnamon Bread

Makes 1 Bundt pan; serves 8 to 12

I always remember this being a go-to breakfast in the morning after a sleepover. The pull-apart Bundt is traditionally sticky, sweet, and buttery, with a touch of cinnamon, but you could alter this recipe to work for a savory pull-apart bread, too—just coat the dough balls in garlic butter or oil before piling them in the pan with shredded cheese in between.

DOUGH

1¾ cups (400 grams) whole milk, warmed

1 (¼-ounce) packet active dry yeast (2¼ teaspoons)

2 tablespoons unsalted butter, melted

1 large egg

1 teaspoon pure vanilla extract

3¼ cups (450 grams) gluten-free 1:1 replacement flour blend

2 tablespoons ground psyllium husk (see page 11)

¼ cup (50 grams) granulated sugar

1½ teaspoons kosher salt

Nonstick cooking spray

COATING

½ cup (100 grams) granulated sugar

1 tablespoon ground cinnamon

¾ cup packed (160 grams) dark brown sugar

½ cup (1 stick) unsalted butter

Pinch of kosher salt

1 **Make the dough:** In a medium bowl or large glass measuring cup, whisk together the milk and yeast. Let stand for 5 minutes, until foamy. Add the melted butter, egg, and vanilla and whisk until combined.

2 In the bowl of a stand mixer fitted with the paddle attachment, combine the flour, psyllium husk, granulated sugar, and salt. With the mixer running on low speed, slowly pour in the wet mixture. Increase the speed to medium-low and beat until a smooth dough forms, about 2 minutes. Shape the dough into a ball at the bottom of the bowl, cover, and let stand until visibly risen and puffy, 1 to 1½ hours.

3 Preheat the oven to 350°F. Coat a Bundt pan with cooking spray.

4 **Make the coating:** In a medium bowl, whisk together the granulated sugar and cinnamon.

5 Pull golf ball–size pieces of dough from the dough ball and roll them into balls, then roll them in the cinnamon-sugar mixture to coat and place them in the prepared pan. Repeat until you have used all the dough.

6 In a medium saucepan, combine the brown sugar, butter, and salt. Cook over medium-high heat, whisking occasionally, until the butter has melted and the sugar has dissolved, about 4 minutes. Pour the mixture into the pan over the dough. Let stand until the dough has risen almost to the top of the pan, about 20 minutes.

7 Bake for about 30 minutes, until golden brown. Remove from the oven and let cool until cool enough to handle, about 30 minutes. Invert the pan onto a plate, remove the pan, and serve immediately.

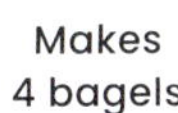

Speedy Bagels

Makes 4 bagels

Inspired by the viral two-ingredient dough, I make these bagels with a homemade "self-rising" flour and Greek yogurt, meaning there is no rising time so they're ready in a jiff. Boiling them before baking gives them that classic bagel chewiness, so don't skip that step!

- 1¼ cups (175 grams) gluten-free 1:1 replacement flour blend, plus more for dusting
- 1 cup (255 grams) plain Greek yogurt
- 1½ teaspoons baking powder
- ¼ teaspoon kosher salt
- 1 tablespoon baking soda
- 1 tablespoon honey or light brown sugar

1 Preheat the oven to 425°F. Line a large baking sheet with parchment paper.

2 In the bowl of a stand mixer fitted with the paddle attachment, combine the flour, yogurt, baking powder, and salt and beat on medium speed until a smooth dough forms. Transfer to a lightly floured surface and knead into a smooth ball.

3 Cut the dough into four equal pieces. Roll each piece into a ball, then poke a hole through the middle and, moving the dough in a circular motion with your thumb and forefingers in the center of the hole, stretch the dough to widen the hole to about 1 inch.

4 In a large pot, combine 4 cups (960 grams) water, the baking soda, and the honey. Bring to a boil over high heat, then reduce the heat to maintain a simmer. Working in batches, if necessary, drop in the bagels and cook until they float, about 1 minute. Using a slotted spoon, transfer the bagels to the prepared baking sheet, shaking off excess water.

5 Bake for about 20 minutes, until browned. Remove from the oven and let cool completely before slicing, about 1 hour. These are best the day they're baked, but can be placed in a resealable plastic bag and frozen for up to 3 months. To reheat, microwave for 1 minute and then toast before serving.

VARIATIONS

SAVORY BAGELS

After boiling the bagels, immediately sprinkle them with toppings such as poppy seeds, sesame seeds, dried minced onion, coarse salt, and/or everything bagel seasoning. Bake as directed.

SWEET BAGELS

After you mix the dough, beat in ½ cup (65 grams) dried blueberries or ½ cup (65 grams) raisins and 1 teaspoon ground cinnamon. Continue with the recipe as directed.

Challah

Makes 1 loaf; serves 12

Challah may just be my favorite thing to bake, and I make it almost every week. Even my daughters know how to braid a loaf of challah now. A gluten-free version has been the most requested recipe over the past few years, and it's finally here! I like to double the recipe so I have one loaf to enjoy right away and a second loaf to use for the bread pudding on page 88.

- 1¼ cups (300 grams) warm water
- 2½ teaspoons (8 grams) active dry yeast
- ¼ cup (50 grams) neutral oil, such as avocado, sunflower, grapeseed, or canola oil
- 3 large eggs: 2 left whole, 1 separated
- 3 cups (415 grams) gluten-free 1:1 replacement flour blend, plus more for dusting
- 2 tablespoons ground psyllium husk (see page 11)
- ¼ cup (50 grams) sugar
- 1½ teaspoons kosher salt

1 In a medium bowl or large glass measuring cup, whisk together the warm water and yeast. Let stand for 5 minutes, until foamy. Add the oil, 2 eggs, and 1 egg yolk (reserve the white) and whisk until combined.

2 In the bowl of a stand mixer fitted with the paddle attachment, combine the flour, psyllium husk, sugar, and salt. With the mixer running on low speed, slowly pour in the wet ingredients. Increase the speed to medium-low and beat until a smooth dough forms.

3 Line a baking sheet with parchment paper. On a lightly floured surface, separate the dough into 3 equal pieces. Roll each piece into a 15-inch-long rope. Lay the ropes next to each other on your work surface and pinch the ends together at the top, then braid the ropes and pinch the ends together at the bottom to seal. Tuck both ends under slightly and push the ends toward each other, tightening up the loaf so it is about 8×5 inches. Transfer it to the prepared baking sheet. Brush with some of the reserved egg white (you will have some egg white left over; store it in the fridge until ready to bake). Cover and let rise until doubled in size, 1 to 1½ hours at room temperature or overnight in the fridge.

4 When ready to bake, preheat the oven to 375°F.

5 Brush the remaining egg white over the dough. Bake for 45 minutes, until golden. Remove from the oven and let cool completely before slicing. Store in an airtight container at room temperature for up to 3 days.

Croissants

Makes
8 croissants

Croissants are a labor of love whether they're gluten-free or not, but they are so worth it! And don't worry if you have leftovers—you can turn day-old croissants into crookies or almond croissants. This is the time to bring out your best butter, since it's the star of the show—opt for a high-fat variety like European butter or cultured butter.

- 1¾ cups (420 grams) warm water
- ¼ cup (50 grams) sugar
- 1 (¼-ounce) packet active dry yeast (2¼ teaspoons)
- 3¼ cups (450 grams) gluten-free 1:1 replacement flour blend, plus more for dusting
- 2 tablespoons ground psyllium husk (see page 11)
- 1½ teaspoons kosher salt
- 1 cup (2 sticks) cold unsalted butter
- 1 large egg yolk
- 1 tablespoon heavy cream

1 In a medium bowl or large glass measuring cup, whisk together the water, sugar, and yeast. Let stand for 5 minutes, until foamy.

2 In the bowl of a stand mixer fitted with the paddle attachment, combine the flour, psyllium husk, and salt. With the mixer running on low speed, slowly pour in the yeast mixture. Add 2 tablespoons of the cold butter, increase the speed to medium-low, and beat until a smooth dough forms. Shape the dough into a ball at the bottom of the bowl and, using a sharp knife or a bread lame, score an "X" in the top of the dough ball. Cover and refrigerate until visibly risen and puffy, 1 to 1½ hours.

3 Meanwhile, place the remaining 14 tablespoons butter in the center of a 16-inch-long piece of parchment paper. Fold the four edges of the parchment paper up over the butter, creating an 8-inch square, and use a rolling pin to pound the butter into a thin layer. Continue rolling and pounding the butter until it fills the entire 8-inch square. Refrigerate until firm, about 20 minutes.

4 On a lightly floured surface, roll the dough out to an 8×16-inch rectangle. Unwrap the butter block and place it in the center of the dough. Fold the top and bottom edges of the dough up over the butter so they meet in the middle of the block. Pinch the dough together where the edges meet and all along the sides to seal so that the butter is encased in the dough. Rotate the dough so the seam is vertical, then roll it out to an 8×16-inch rectangle. Fold the bottom edge of the dough up to the center, then fold the top edge down to the center so they meet, and finally fold the entire thing in half so you have four layers. Wrap the dough in plastic wrap and refrigerate for 1 hour.

5 Place the dough back on the lightly floured surface with one short side closest to you. Roll the dough out to an 8×16-inch rectangle and repeat the same folding process: Fold the bottom edge of the dough up to the center, then fold the top edge down to the center so they meet, and finally fold the entire thing in half. Wrap the dough in plastic and refrigerate for 1 hour.

Recipe continues

6 Line two baking sheets with parchment paper.

7 Place the dough back on the lightly floured surface and roll it out to an 8×16-inch rectangle. Using a pizza cutter or sharp knife, trim the edges of the dough so you have straight, clean edges, then cut the dough into four 4×8-inch rectangles. Cut each rectangle in half diagonally so you have 8 triangles. Working with one triangle at a time, stretch the two corners of the long edge of the dough away from each other to center out the triangle. Then, starting at that long edge, roll the dough up into a croissant. Transfer the croissant to one of the prepared baking sheets, point-side down, and repeat with the remaining dough. Cover with a clean kitchen towel and let rise at room temperature until visibly puffy, 2 to 2½ hours, then place the dough in the freezer for 30 minutes.

8 Arrange two oven racks so one is in the upper middle position and the other is in the lower middle. Preheat the oven to 375°F.

9 Remove the croissants from the freezer and uncover them. In a small bowl, whisk together the egg yolk and cream. Brush the mixture over the croissants. Bake for about 40 minutes, switching racks and rotating the pans from front to back once halfway through, until flaky and browned. Serve warm, or let cool completely and store in an airtight container at room temperature for up to 2 days. Reheat before serving.

VARIATIONS

CROOKIES

Preheat the oven to 350°F. Cut day-old croissants in half horizontally and fill the centers with chocolate chip cookie dough (see page 40). Place them on a baking sheet and bake for about 15 minutes, until the cookie dough is set and golden.

ALMOND CROISSANTS

Preheat the oven to 350°F. Beat 4 tablespoons (½ stick) room-temperature unsalted butter with ¼ cup (50 grams) sugar, 1 large egg, ½ teaspoon pure almond extract, ½ cup (50 grams) almond flour, and a pinch of kosher salt. Cut 4 day-old croissants in half horizontally and fill the centers with the almond mixture. Place the croissants on a baking sheet and brush the tops with orgeat (or make a simple syrup with equal parts sugar and water, flavor the syrup with some almond extract, and use that for brushing instead). Sprinkle with sliced almonds. Bake for about 15 minutes, until the almond filling is set and golden.

Sourdough Bread

Makes
1 sourdough starter
and 1 loaf sourdough
bread

Once you make this bread, you won't want to go back to store-bought. It's crisp on the outside but soft and chewy on the inside, just like sourdough should be—but entirely gluten-free. Don't be intimidated by the process, it's easier than it sounds and so worth it.

STARTER

Gluten-free 1:1 replacement flour blend

Filtered water

BREAD

2 tablespoons ground psyllium husk (see page 11)

2¼ cups (530 grams) warm water

3 cups (400 grams) gluten-free 1:1 replacement flour blend, plus more for dusting

1 tablespoon honey or pure maple syrup

1 tablespoon kosher salt

1 **Make the starter:** In a clean pint-size glass jar, stir together 30 grams of flour and 40 grams of filtered water. Loosely cover and let stand at room temperature for 24 hours.

2 Transfer 15 grams of the starter to a clean pint-size glass jar (discard the starter remaining in the first jar) and stir in 30 grams of flour and 40 grams of filtered water. Loosely cover and let stand at room temperature for 24 hours. Repeat this step until the starter is very bubbly and doubles in size after resting for 24 hours, about 6 days total.

3 Transfer 30 grams of the bubbly starter to a clean quart-size glass jar (discard the starter remaining in the first jar) and stir in 60 grams of flour and 80 grams of filtered water. Loosely cover and let stand at room temperature until doubled in size, 8 to 12 hours.

4 Transfer 15 grams of the starter to a clean pint-size glass jar (reserve the remaining starter for the bread dough) and stir in 30 grams of flour and 40 grams of filtered water. Cover and refrigerate for future use (if storing the starter for longer than a week, take the jar out once a week and repeat this step to feed the starter).

5 **Make the bread:** In the bowl of a stand mixer fitted with the paddle attachment, whisk together the psyllium husk and warm water until a thick gel forms. Add the flour, honey, salt, and the reserved bubbly starter and mix on low speed until a smooth dough forms. Shape the dough into a ball at the bottom of the bowl, cover, and let rise at room temperature until visibly puffy, 2 to 4 hours.

6 Line a proofing basket or large bowl with a tea towel and lightly dust with flour.

7 Dump the dough out onto a lightly floured work surface and gently knead and flatten it into a 1-inch-thick disc. *If making a round loaf,* fold the four edges into the center and flip it over so it's seam-side down. Gently push and roll the loaf counterclockwise against the work surface while keeping the ball seam-side down to tighten the ball and smooth out the seam. Transfer the

Recipe continues

dough to the prepared proofing basket or bowl. *If making an oblong loaf,* roll the disc up into a log (like a jelly roll), then pick it up folding it in half horizontally so the ends meet. Place it into the prepared proofing basket like that, seam-side up, and pinch the seam to seal. Cover the loaf and refrigerate until domed and puffy, at least 8 hours or up to 12 hours.

8 Preheat the oven to 500°F. Place a 5-quart or larger Dutch oven in the oven to preheat as well.

9 Crumple up a piece of parchment paper under running water to dampen it. Flatten out the parchment and flip the dough out onto it. Using a sharp knife or a bread lame, score the top of the loaf with at least one large slash. Using the parchment, lift the dough and carefully lower it into the hot Dutch oven. Cover with the lid and bake for 20 minutes. Reduce the oven temperature to 425°F and bake for 40 minutes, then uncover and bake for 20 minutes more, until golden. Remove from the oven and let cool completely before slicing. Store in an airtight container at room temperature for up to 3 days.

Cranberry-Orange Scones

Makes
8 scones

These tangy scones get a double dose of orange with zest in the dough as well as zest and juice in the glaze. I like to use frozen cranberries because they're easy to find year-round, but if you have fresh ones, they'll work just as well.

- 2 cups (275 grams) gluten-free 1:1 replacement flour blend, plus more for dusting
- ½ cup (100 grams) granulated sugar
- 1 tablespoon baking powder
- Zest of 1 large orange
- ½ teaspoon kosher salt
- ½ cup (1 stick) unsalted butter, frozen
- ¾ cup (125 grams) buttermilk
- 1 teaspoon pure vanilla extract
- 1 cup (120 grams) frozen cranberries
- 1 tablespoon heavy cream
- 2 cups (225 grams) powdered sugar
- ¼ cup (60 grams) fresh orange juice

1 Preheat the oven to 400°F. Line a large baking sheet with parchment paper.

2 In a large bowl, whisk together the flour, granulated sugar, baking powder, half the orange zest, and the salt. Using the large holes of a box grater, grate the cold butter directly into the dry ingredients. Toss it all together so the butter is completely coated with the dry ingredients.

3 In a medium bowl, whisk together the buttermilk and vanilla. Make a well in the dry ingredients, then pour the wet ingredients into the well and stir together to form a scraggly dough. Add the cranberries and knead into a cohesive ball.

4 Turn the dough out onto a floured surface and pat it out into an 8-inch-wide round. Cut the dough round into 8 equal triangles and place them on the prepared baking sheet, spacing them about 1 inch apart. Brush the tops with the cream. Bake for about 20 minutes, until golden brown.

5 Meanwhile, in a medium bowl, whisk together the powdered sugar, orange juice, and remaining orange zest until smooth.

6 Remove the scones from the oven and let cool on the pan for about 10 minutes, then transfer to a wire rack set over a rimmed baking sheet and drizzle with the glaze. These are best the day they're made.

Apple Cinnamon Baked Oats

Makes one 8-inch pan; serves 9

Think of this like an apple crisp that you can eat for breakfast! I love it topped with a big dollop of vanilla Greek yogurt for some added protein that mimics the scoop of ice cream you would serve atop apple crumble.

- Nonstick cooking spray
- 4 cups (495 grams) gluten-free rolled oats
- 3 cups (685 grams) whole milk
- 2 medium apples (370 grams), cored and diced
- 1 cup (255 grams) unsweetened applesauce
- ¼ cup (80 grams) pure maple syrup
- 1 tablespoon ground cinnamon
- 1 teaspoon pure vanilla extract
- ½ teaspoon kosher salt
- 1 cup (140 grams) gluten-free 1:1 replacement flour blend
- ½ cup packed (105 grams) light brown sugar
- ½ cup (1 stick) unsalted butter, melted

1 Preheat the oven to 350°F. Coat an 8-inch baking dish with cooking spray.

2 In a large bowl, stir together 3 cups (370 grams) of the oats, the milk, apples, applesauce, maple syrup, cinnamon, and vanilla. Pour the mixture into the prepared pan.

3 In a small bowl, stir together the remaining 1 cup (125 grams) oats, the salt, flour, and brown sugar. Drizzle in the melted butter and stir to combine until clumps form. Sprinkle clumps of the crumble mixture over the top of the oat mixture. Bake for about 45 minutes, until the oatmeal is tender and the topping is golden.

4 Store, covered, in the refrigerator for up to 3 days. Reheat before serving.

BARS

Rainbow Chocolate Chip Granola Bars

Makes
16 bars

When packing my kids' lunches, I always include a protein, a vegetable, and a treat. They love finding these bars as the treat in their lunch boxes, and I love that it's a treat chock-full of healthy ingredients that will actually fill them up. I make them with sunflower seed butter to keep them nut-free and school-safe, but feel free to swap in your favorite nut butter.

- Nonstick cooking spray
- 3 cups (370 grams) gluten-free rolled oats
- 2¼ cups (385 grams) mini rainbow chocolate nonpareils
- 1 cup (45 grams) gluten-free crisped rice cereal
- 1 cup (55 grams) unsweetened shredded coconut
- ¼ teaspoon kosher salt
- ⅔ cup (240 grams) brown rice syrup
- ½ cup (130 grams) creamy sunflower seed butter, almond butter, or peanut butter
- ⅓ cup (75 grams) coconut oil
- 1 teaspoon pure vanilla extract

1 Preheat the oven to 325°F. Line a 9×13-inch baking pan with parchment paper, leaving some overhang on the two long sides. Lightly coat the parchment with cooking spray.

2 In a large bowl, combine the oats, 2 cups (340 grams) of the nonpareils, the cereal, shredded coconut, and salt.

3 Place the brown rice syrup, sunflower seed butter, coconut oil, and vanilla in a medium microwave-safe bowl and microwave on high in 30-second intervals, stirring after each, until the coconut oil is melted, about 1 minute. Stir to combine. Let stand until cool to the touch, about 5 minutes, then pour the mixture over the dry ingredients in the large bowl and stir to coat.

4 Press the mixture into the prepared pan in an even layer and sprinkle the remaining ¼ cup (45 grams) nonpareils over the top. Bake for about 20 minutes, until the edges start to brown. Remove from the oven and let cool until cool enough to handle, about 15 minutes, then use the overhanging parchment to transfer the bars to a cutting board. Cut into 16 bars, leaving them together on the cutting board, and let cool completely before separating the bars, about 1 hour.

5 Store in an airtight container at room temperature for up to 1 week.

GO FOR GRANOLA

To make granola instead of granola bars, bake the mixture until the top is lightly browned, about 30 minutes. Let the granola cool completely, then break it up into chunks to serve over yogurt, etc. Store in an airtight container at room temperature for up to 1 week.

S’mores Brownies

Makes 16 brownies

This is truly the next best thing to a hot, fresh-from-the-fire s’more. I use a combination of Marshmallow Fluff and mini marshmallows to give them that gooey texture, even if you aren’t eating them warm from the oven.

Nonstick cooking spray

1¼ cups (215 grams) semisweet chocolate chips

½ cup (1 stick) unsalted butter

¾ cup (150 grams) sugar

2 large eggs

1 teaspoon pure vanilla extract

1 cup (140 grams) gluten-free 1:1 replacement flour blend

½ teaspoon baking powder

½ teaspoon kosher salt

6 sheets gluten-free graham crackers (100 grams), broken into bite-size pieces

½ cup (65 grams) Marshmallow Fluff

1 cup (55 grams) mini marshmallows

1 (1½-ounce) milk chocolate bar, such as Hershey’s, broken into pieces

1 Preheat the oven to 350°F. Line an 8-inch square baking pan with parchment paper, leaving some overhang on two sides. Lightly coat the pan and parchment with cooking spray.

2 Place 1 cup (170 grams) of the chocolate chips and the butter in a medium microwave-safe bowl and microwave in 30-second intervals, stirring after each, until completely melted and smooth. Add the sugar and whisk thoroughly to combine. Add the eggs one at a time and whisk until smooth. Whisk in the vanilla.

3 In a medium bowl, whisk together the flour, baking powder, and salt. Fold the dry ingredients into the chocolate mixture. Fold in the remaining ¼ cup (45 grams) chocolate chips and half the graham cracker pieces.

4 Transfer the batter to the prepared pan. Dollop the Fluff onto the batter and swirl it in to slightly incorporate it. Bake for about 25 minutes, until the top is set and a toothpick inserted into the center of the brownies comes out with just a few moist crumbs attached. Remove the pan from the oven and turn the broiler on high.

5 Evenly scatter the mini marshmallows, remaining graham cracker pieces, and the chocolate bar pieces over the brownies. Broil for about 20 seconds, until the marshmallows are lightly toasted. Remove from the oven and let cool completely, about 1 hour. Use the overhanging parchment to transfer the brownies to a cutting board and cut into squares. Store in an airtight container at room temperature for up to 4 days.

Scotcheroos

Makes
24 bars

Being a born-and-raised New Yorker, I'd never even heard of scotcheroos until a Midwestern friend of mine brought them to a party. One bite of the crispy, peanut buttery, chocolaty, butterscotch-y treat, and I was hooked! If you're a chocolate lover like me, you can swap out the crisped rice cereal for cocoa crispies.

- Nonstick cooking spray
- 1 cup (310 grams) light corn syrup
- 1 cup (200 grams) sugar
- 4 tablespoons (½ stick) unsalted butter
- 1 cup (255 grams) creamy peanut butter
- 6 cups (260 grams) gluten-free crisped rice cereal
- 2 cups (340 grams) semisweet chocolate chips
- 2 cups (340 grams) butterscotch chips
- 1 teaspoon coconut oil

1 Line a 9×13-inch baking pan with parchment paper, leaving some overhang on the two long sides. Lightly coat the pan and parchment with cooking spray.

2 In a large saucepan, combine the corn syrup, sugar, and butter and cook over medium-high heat, whisking, until the butter has melted, the sugar has dissolved, and the mixture just barely starts to boil. Remove from the heat and stir in the peanut butter until smooth and melted. Add the cereal and stir to coat. Press the mixture into the prepared pan in an even layer.

3 Place the chocolate chips and 1½ cups (255 grams) of the butterscotch chips in a large microwave-safe bowl and microwave in 30-second intervals, whisking after each, until melted and smooth. Spread the mixture in an even layer over the cereal mixture in the pan.

4 Place the remaining ½ cup (85 grams) butterscotch chips and the coconut oil in a small microwave-safe bowl and microwave in 30-second intervals, whisking after each, until melted and smooth.

5 Transfer the butterscotch mixture to a plastic bag and snip off one corner. Pipe parallel lines of the butterscotch mixture on top of the chocolate mixture in the pan. Run a knife perpendicular to the butterscotch lines, doing every other one in the opposite direction. Refrigerate the bars until the chocolate and butterscotch are set, about 1 hour. Use the overhanging parchment to transfer the scotcheroos to a cutting board and cut into bars. Store in an airtight container at room temperature for up to 1 week.

Brown Butter Rice Crispy Treats

Makes 18 bars

I like my rice crispy treats dense and compact. To achieve that perfect texture, try spraying a piece of parchment paper with nonstick cooking spray, laying it on top of the bars in the pan, and using it to press down firmly and smooth out the mixture.

Nonstick cooking spray

4 tablespoons (½ stick) unsalted butter

8 cups (440 grams) mini marshmallows

6 cups (260 grams) gluten-free crisped rice cereal

1 Line a 9 × 13-inch baking pan with parchment paper, leaving some overhang on the two long sides. Lightly coat the pan and parchment with cooking spray.

2 Melt the butter in a large saucepan over medium-high heat, then cook, swirling the pan occasionally to prevent the butter from bubbling over, until brown flecks begin to form, about 5 minutes. Add 6 cups (330 grams) of the marshmallows and cook, stirring continuously, until the marshmallows have melted and the mixture is smooth. Remove the pan from the heat and stir in the cereal until coated.

3 Stir the remaining 2 cups (110 grams) marshmallows into the cereal mixture. Transfer the mixture to the prepared baking pan and press it into an even layer (see headnote). Let cool completely, about 30 minutes. Use the overhanging parchment to transfer to a cutting board and cut into bars. Store in an airtight container at room temperature for up to 1 week.

VARIATIONS

FRUITY RICE CRISPY TREATS

Place the butter and 6 cups (330 grams) marshmallows in a large microwave-safe bowl and microwave in 30-second intervals, stirring after each, until fully melted and smooth. Stir in 6 cups (260 grams) fruity gluten-free crisped rice cereal and continue with the recipe as written.

COOKIES & CREAM RICE CRISPY TREATS

Place the butter and 6 cups (330 grams) marshmallows in a large microwave-safe bowl and microwave in 30-second intervals, stirring after each, until fully melted and smooth. Stir in 4 cups (175 grams) gluten-free cocoa-flavored crisped rice cereal and 2 cups (85 grams) gluten-free crisped rice cereal and continue with the recipe as written, stirring 10 crushed gluten-free chocolate sandwich cookies (such as gluten-free Oreos; 110 grams) into the mixture along with the remaining 2 cups (110 grams) marshmallows in step 3.

Oreo Cheesecake Bars

Makes 16 bars

The release of gluten-free Oreos in 2021 opened up a whole new world of gluten-free baked goods. Here I use them to make cookies-and-cream cheesecake bars with a thick cookie crust.

- Nonstick cooking spray
- 1 (12-ounce) package gluten-free Oreos (about 30 cookies)
- 4 tablespoons (½ stick) unsalted butter, melted
- 2 (8-ounce) blocks full-fat cream cheese, at room temperature
- ⅔ cup (130 grams) sugar
- 2 large eggs
- ½ cup (115 grams) heavy cream
- 1 tablespoon fresh lemon juice
- 1 teaspoon pure vanilla extract
- ½ teaspoon kosher salt

1 Preheat the oven to 325°F. Line a 9-inch square baking pan with parchment paper, leaving some overhang on two sides. Coat the pan and parchment with cooking spray.

2 Place two-thirds of the Oreos (about 20 cookies) in a food processor and pulse until finely ground. With the motor running, drizzle in the melted butter until the Oreos start to clump together. Press the Oreo mixture into an even layer over the bottom of the prepared pan.

3 Wipe out the food processor, then combine the cream cheese, sugar, eggs, heavy cream, lemon juice, vanilla, and salt and process until thoroughly combined and smooth. Pour the cream cheese mixture over the crust in the pan. Crush the remaining Oreos into pieces and sprinkle them over the cream cheese mixture.

4 Bake for about 50 minutes, until set on top but still jiggly in the center. Remove from the oven and let cool for at least 1 hour, then refrigerate until chilled, about 4 hours.

5 Run a butter knife around the edges of the pan and use the overhanging parchment to transfer the cheesecake to a cutting board. Cut the cheesecake into 16 bars. Store in an airtight container in the refrigerator for up to 3 days.

Frosted Sugar Cookie Bars

Makes 16 bars

When I was a kid, a super-soft sugar cookie topped with a thick layer of buttercream frosting from the grocery store bakery was my all-time favorite treat. I adorn these cookie bars with pale pink frosting and rainbow sprinkles as an homage to the ones I enjoyed throughout my childhood. But these are honestly so much better than anything you can buy. Feel free to leave out the food coloring and sprinkles—the bars will be less colorful but just as tasty.

BARS

Nonstick cooking spray

2½ cups (345 grams) gluten-free 1:1 replacement flour blend

1 teaspoon baking powder

½ teaspoon kosher salt

1 cup (2 sticks) unsalted butter, at room temperature

1½ cups (300 grams) granulated sugar

2 large eggs

2 teaspoons pure vanilla extract

FROSTING

1 cup (2 sticks) unsalted butter, at room temperature

4 cups (455 grams) powdered sugar

2 tablespoons whole milk

1 teaspoon pure vanilla extract

1 drop pink gel food coloring

Sprinkles, for garnish

1 **Make the bars:** Preheat the oven to 350°F. Line a 9 × 13-inch baking pan with parchment paper, leaving some overhang on the two long sides. Lightly coat the pan and parchment with cooking spray.

2 In a medium bowl, whisk together the flour, baking powder, and salt.

3 In the bowl of a stand mixer fitted with the paddle attachment, beat the butter and granulated sugar on medium-high speed until light and fluffy, about 3 minutes. Add the eggs one at a time and beat until smooth. Beat in the vanilla. With the mixer on low, gradually add the dry ingredients and beat until fully incorporated.

4 Transfer the mixture to the prepared pan and smooth it into an even layer. Bake for about 20 minutes, until set on top and golden on the edges. Remove from the oven and let cool completely, about 2 hours, then use the overhanging parchment to transfer the cookie block to a cutting board.

5 **Make the frosting:** In the bowl of a stand mixer fitted with the whisk attachment, combine the butter, powdered sugar, milk, vanilla, and food coloring and beat on medium speed until combined. Scrape down the sides of the bowl and beat on high until light and fluffy, 2 to 5 minutes.

6 Spread the frosting over the cooled cookie block, decorate with sprinkles, then cut it into squares. Store in an airtight container at room temperature for up to 4 days.

Cheesecake Swirl Brownies

Makes 16 brownies

Whenever my husband and I go out to dinner, there is one thing we can never agree on: what to get for dessert. Adam always opts for something chocolate, while all I want is cheesecake. I developed this recipe to be our perfect dessert compromise. Now that I've made them, I know you should absolutely be pairing cheesecake and brownies. It just tastes better!

BROWNIE BATTER

- Nonstick cooking spray
- 1 cup (140 grams) gluten-free 1:1 replacement flour blend
- ½ teaspoon baking powder
- ½ teaspoon kosher salt
- 1 cup (170 grams) semisweet chocolate chips
- ½ cup (1 stick) unsalted butter
- ¾ cup (150 grams) sugar
- 2 large eggs
- 1 teaspoon pure vanilla extract

CHEESECAKE SWIRL

- 1 (8-ounce) block full-fat cream cheese, at room temperature
- ½ cup (100 grams) sugar
- ¼ cup (35 grams) gluten-free 1:1 replacement flour blend
- 1 large egg
- 1 teaspoon pure vanilla extract

1 **Make the brownie batter:** Preheat the oven to 350°F. Line an 8-inch square baking pan with parchment paper, leaving some overhang on two sides. Lightly coat the pan and parchment with cooking spray.

2 In a medium bowl, whisk together the flour, baking powder, and salt.

3 Place the chocolate chips and the butter in a large microwave-safe bowl and microwave in 30-second intervals, stirring after each, until completely melted and smooth. Add the sugar and whisk thoroughly to combine. Add the eggs one at a time and whisk until smooth. Whisk in the vanilla. Fold the dry ingredients into the chocolate mixture until combined.

4 **Make the cheesecake swirl:** In a large bowl, combine the cream cheese, sugar, flour, egg, and vanilla and beat with a handheld mixer on medium speed until smooth.

5 Spread half the brownie batter into the prepared pan. Dollop half the cheesecake mixture on top and, using a knife, swirl them together, being careful not to overmix. Spread the remaining brownie batter on top, dollop with the remaining cheesecake mixture, and swirl them together.

6 Bake for about 30 minutes, until the top is set and a toothpick inserted into the center of the brownies comes out with just a few moist crumbs attached. Remove from the oven and let cool completely, about 1 hour.

7 Use the overhanging parchment to transfer the brownies to a cutting board and cut into squares. Store in an airtight container in the refrigerator for up to 3 days.

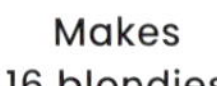

Chocolate Chunk Brown Butter Blondies

Makes
16 blondies

I love a good thick-and-chewy chocolate chip cookie, but to achieve that texture, you usually have to refrigerate the dough for a long period of time to ensure the cookies don't spread too far while they're baking. Blondies are the perfect solution for that. The pan keeps everything contained, giving you crispy edges and that perfect chewy center with no refrigeration time needed.

- Nonstick cooking spray
- 2 cups (275 grams) gluten-free 1:1 replacement flour blend
- 1 teaspoon baking powder
- ½ teaspoon baking soda
- ½ teaspoon kosher salt
- 1 cup (2 sticks) unsalted butter
- ¾ cup packed (160 grams) light brown sugar
- ¾ cup (150 grams) granulated sugar
- 2 large eggs
- 1 teaspoon pure vanilla extract
- 1 (6-ounce) dark chocolate bar, chopped (about 2 cups)
- Flaky sea salt, for sprinkling (optional)

1 Preheat the oven to 350°F. Line a 9-inch square baking pan with parchment paper, leaving some overhang on two sides. Lightly coat the pan and parchment with cooking spray.

2 In a medium bowl, whisk together the flour, baking powder, baking soda, and salt.

3 Melt the butter in a large saucepan over medium-high heat, then cook, swirling the pan occasionally to prevent the butter from bubbling over, until brown flecks begin to form, about 5 minutes. Transfer the melted butter to a large heatproof bowl and whisk in the brown sugar and granulated sugar. Add the eggs one at a time and whisk until smooth. Whisk in the vanilla. Stir in the dry ingredients, then fold in the chopped chocolate.

4 Transfer the batter to the prepared pan and smooth it into an even layer. Sprinkle with flaky salt, if desired. Bake for about 25 minutes, until set on top and golden on the edges. Remove from the oven and let cool completely, about 1 hour. Use the overhanging parchment to transfer the blondies to a cutting board and cut into squares. Store in an airtight container at room temperature for up to 4 days.

Peach Crumble Bars

Makes 12 bars

Peach crumble may be a classic dessert, but given the choice, I will always choose a bar over a crisp. Bars last longer, are easier to store and to serve, and are so much prettier. Plus, with my recipe, they're just as easy. I make one mixture that acts as both the crust and the crumble topping. For even more flavor in this treat, try browning the butter. Just melt the butter in a small saucepan over medium-high heat, stirring occasionally, until brown flecks appear and it begins to smell nutty, about 5 minutes. Allow the butter to cool slightly before adding it to the flour mixture.

- Nonstick cooking spray
- 2½ cups (345 grams) gluten-free 1:1 replacement flour blend
- 2½ cups (310 grams) gluten-free rolled oats
- 1 cup packed (210 grams) light brown sugar
- 1 teaspoon ground cardamom
- 1 teaspoon kosher salt
- 1½ cups (3 sticks) unsalted butter, melted
- 4 large peaches (about 2 pounds), pitted and sliced (about 7 cups)
- ½ cup (100 grams) granulated sugar
- ¼ cup (30 grams) cornstarch
- 1 tablespoon fresh lemon juice
- 1 teaspoon pure vanilla extract

1 Preheat the oven to 350°F. Line a 9×13-inch baking dish with parchment paper, leaving some overhang on the two long sides. Coat the dish and parchment with cooking spray.

2 In a medium bowl, whisk together the flour, oats, brown sugar, cardamom, and salt. Add the melted butter and stir to combine. Transfer 2 cups of the mixture to a separate medium bowl and set aside. Press the remaining mixture into the prepared baking dish.

3 In a large bowl, combine the peaches, granulated sugar, cornstarch, lemon juice, and vanilla and toss to evenly coat the peaches. Pour the peaches over the crust and crumble the reserved oat mixture over the peaches.

4 Bake for about 1 hour, until the top is golden and the filling is bubbling. Remove from the oven and let cool completely, about 1 hour. Use the overhanging parchment to transfer the peach crumble to a cutting board, then cut into 12 bars.

5 Store in an airtight container in the refrigerator for up to 3 days.

Chocolate Mint Brownies

Makes 16 brownies

These are like an Andes mint in brownie form. I add a touch of butter to the ganache to ensure it stays nice and soft so the mint buttercream doesn't all smoosh out the sides with every bite.

BROWNIES

- Nonstick cooking spray
- 1 cup (140 grams) gluten-free 1:1 replacement flour blend
- ½ teaspoon baking powder
- ½ teaspoon kosher salt
- 1 cup (170 grams) semisweet chocolate chips
- ½ cup (1 stick) unsalted butter
- ¾ cup (150 grams) granulated sugar
- 2 large eggs
- 1 teaspoon pure vanilla extract

MINT FROSTING

- ½ cup (1 stick) unsalted butter, at room temperature
- 2 cups (225 grams) powdered sugar
- 1 tablespoon whole milk
- 1 teaspoon peppermint extract
- 1 drop green gel food coloring

GANACHE

- 1½ cups (255 grams) semisweet chocolate chips
- 2 tablespoons unsalted butter, cut into small cubes
- ½ cup (115 grams) heavy cream

1 **Make the brownies:** Preheat the oven to 350°F. Line an 8-inch square baking pan with parchment paper, leaving some overhang on two sides. Lightly coat the pan and parchment with cooking spray.

2 In a medium bowl, whisk together the flour, baking powder, and salt.

3 Place the chocolate chips and the butter in a medium microwave-safe bowl and microwave in 30-second intervals, stirring after each, until completely melted and smooth. Add the granulated sugar and whisk thoroughly to combine. Add the eggs one at a time and whisk until smooth. Whisk in the vanilla. Fold the dry ingredients into the chocolate mixture.

4 Transfer the batter to the prepared pan. Bake for about 25 minutes, until the top is set and a toothpick inserted into the center comes out with just a few wet crumbs attached. Remove from the oven and let cool completely, about 1 hour.

5 **Make the frosting:** In the bowl of a stand mixer fitted with the whisk attachment, beat the butter, powdered sugar, milk, peppermint extract, and food coloring on medium speed until combined. Scrape down the sides of the bowl and beat on high until fluffy, 2 to 5 minutes. Spread the frosting evenly over the cooled brownies.

6 **Make the ganache:** Place the chocolate chips and butter in a small heatproof bowl or a large glass measuring cup. In a small saucepan, heat the cream over medium-high heat just until it comes to a boil. Pour the hot cream over the chocolate chips and butter in the bowl and let stand for 1 minute, then whisk until smooth. Spread the ganache over the frosted brownies in the pan. Refrigerate until the ganache hardens, about 1 hour.

7 Use the overhanging parchment to transfer the brownies to a cutting board and cut into squares. Store the brownies in an airtight container in the refrigerator for up to 3 days.

CUPCAKES

Strawberry Cheesecake Cupcakes

Makes
12 cupcakes

Roasting strawberries concentrates their flavor and color to give these cupcakes a bright pink hue and intense strawberry flavor. Once baked, the color darkens, so if you want a bright pink, don't skip the food coloring. For even more flair, dust the frosted cupcakes with ground freeze-dried strawberries or sprinkles.

CUPCAKES

- 1 pound fresh strawberries, halved (quartered, if large)
- 1¼ cups (175 grams) gluten-free 1:1 replacement flour blend
- 1½ teaspoons baking powder
- ½ teaspoon kosher salt
- 6 tablespoons (¾ stick) unsalted butter, at room temperature
- 1 cup (200 grams) granulated sugar
- 2 large eggs
- ½ cup (130 grams) plain full-fat Greek yogurt
- 1 teaspoon pure vanilla extract
- 2 or 3 drops red gel food coloring

FROSTING

- ½ cup (1 stick) unsalted butter, at room temperature
- 1 (8-ounce) block full-fat cream cheese, at room temperature
- 4 cups (455 grams) powdered sugar
- 1 tablespoon fresh lemon juice

1 **Make the cupcakes:** Preheat the oven to 350°F. Line a rimmed baking sheet with parchment paper. Line a 12-cup muffin tin with cupcake liners.

2 Spread the strawberries over the prepared baking sheet. Roast for about 40 minutes, stirring once, until the berries have darkened and there aren't any juices left on the pan. Transfer the berries to a food processor or blender and puree until smooth. Keep the oven on.

3 In a medium bowl, whisk together the flour, baking powder, and salt.

4 In the bowl of a stand mixer fitted with the paddle attachment or in a large bowl using a handheld mixer, beat the butter and granulated sugar on medium speed until fluffy, about 2 minutes. Add the eggs one at a time, beating until smooth after each addition. Add the strawberry puree and beat until combined. Beat in the yogurt and vanilla until combined. Add the dry ingredients and beat until smooth, scraping down the bowl as needed. Add the food coloring as needed to reach the desired pink color.

5 Divide the batter evenly among the prepared muffin cups. Bake for about 20 minutes, until lightly golden on top. Remove from the oven and transfer to a wire rack to cool completely, about 1 hour.

6 **Make the frosting:** In the bowl of a stand mixer fitted with the whisk attachment or in a large bowl using a handheld mixer, combine the butter, cream cheese, powdered sugar, and lemon juice and beat on medium speed until combined. Scrape down the sides of the bowl and beat on high until light and fluffy, 2 to 5 minutes. Pipe or spread the frosting on top of the cooled cupcakes. Refrigerate until ready to serve, up to 3 days.

Cookies & Cream Cupcakes

Makes 12 cupcakes

If Oreos in the cake and the frosting is still not enough for you, top each cupcake with a halved cookie.

CUPCAKES

1½ cups (205 grams) gluten-free 1:1 replacement flour blend

1½ teaspoons baking powder

½ teaspoon kosher salt

3 tablespoons unsalted butter, at room temperature

3 tablespoons neutral oil, such as avocado, sunflower, grapeseed, or canola oil

1 cup (200 grams) granulated sugar

2 large eggs

1 teaspoon pure vanilla extract

⅓ cup (75 grams) whole milk

15 gluten-free chocolate sandwich cookies, such as gluten-free Oreos (170 grams)

FROSTING

1½ cups (3 sticks) unsalted butter, at room temperature

6 cups (680 grams) powdered sugar

3 tablespoons whole milk

2 teaspoons pure vanilla extract

15 gluten-free chocolate sandwich cookies, such as gluten-free Oreos (170 grams)

1 **Make the cupcakes:** Preheat the oven to 350°F. Line a 12-cup muffin tin with cupcake liners.

2 In a medium bowl, combine the flour, baking powder, and salt.

3 In the bowl of a stand mixer fitted with the paddle attachment or in a large bowl using a handheld mixer, combine the butter, oil, and granulated sugar and beat on medium speed until fluffy, about 2 minutes. Add the eggs one at a time, beating until smooth after each addition. Beat in the vanilla. Add the dry ingredients in three additions, alternating with the milk, and beat until smooth. Crumble the cookies into large chunks into the bowl and beat until the pieces are evenly distributed throughout the batter.

4 Divide the batter evenly among the prepared muffin cups. Bake for about 25 minutes, until a toothpick inserted into the center comes out with just a few moist crumbs attached. Remove from the oven and transfer to a wire rack to cool completely, about 1 hour.

5 **Make the frosting:** In the bowl of a stand mixer fitted with the whisk attachment or in a large bowl using a handheld mixer, beat the butter, powdered sugar, milk, and vanilla on medium speed until combined. Scrape down the sides of the bowl and beat on high until light and fluffy, 2 to 5 minutes. Transfer one-third of the frosting to a piping bag or small bowl.

6 In a food processor, pulse the cookies into coarse crumbs. Add the cookie crumbs to the mixer bowl with the larger portion of frosting and beat until they are evenly distributed.

7 Use a melon baller or round 1-tablespoon measuring spoon to scoop out a bit of the center of each cupcake, making a well. Fill the wells with the plain frosting, then spread or pipe the cookie frosting on top of each cupcake. Store in an airtight container at room temperature for up to 3 days.

Lemon Cupcakes

Makes
12 cupcakes

A dollop of lemon curd on top of these cupcakes adds a touch of bright color and extra tangy flavor. You can buy store-bought curd or use the recipe on page 173. Want to take the lemon garnish to the next level? Thinly slice a lemon and simmer the slices in a nonstick skillet with equal parts sugar and water until translucent. Drain the slices and let them cool, then place one on top of each cupcake.

CUPCAKES

1½ cups (205 grams) gluten-free 1:1 replacement flour blend

1½ teaspoons baking powder

½ teaspoon kosher salt

3 tablespoons unsalted butter, at room temperature

3 tablespoons neutral oil, such as avocado, sunflower, grapeseed, or canola oil

1 cup (200 grams) granulated sugar

Zest of 1 lemon (about 2 teaspoons)

2 large eggs

1 teaspoon pure vanilla extract

⅓ cup (75 grams) whole milk

FROSTING

1 cup (2 sticks) unsalted butter, at room temperature

4 cups (455 grams) powdered sugar

Zest of 1 lemon (about 2 teaspoons)

1 tablespoon fresh lemon juice

1 teaspoon pure vanilla extract

¾ cup (240 grams) lemon curd (see headnote)

1 **Make the cupcakes:** Preheat the oven to 350°F. Line a 12-cup muffin tin with cupcake liners.

2 In a medium bowl, combine the flour, baking powder, and salt.

3 In the bowl of a stand mixer fitted with the paddle attachment or in a large bowl using a handheld mixer, combine the butter, oil, granulated sugar, and lemon zest and beat on medium speed until fluffy, about 2 minutes. Add the eggs one at a time, beating until smooth after each addition. Beat in the vanilla. Add the dry ingredients in three additions, alternating with the milk, and beat until smooth.

4 Divide the batter evenly among the prepared muffin cups. Bake for about 20 minutes, until a toothpick inserted into the center comes out with just a few moist crumbs attached. Remove from the oven and transfer to a wire rack to cool completely, about 1 hour.

5 **Meanwhile, make the frosting:** In the bowl of a stand mixer fitted with the whisk attachment or in a large bowl using a handheld mixer, combine the butter, powdered sugar, lemon zest, lemon juice, and vanilla and beat on medium speed until combined. Scrape down the sides of the bowl and beat on high until light and fluffy, 2 to 5 minutes.

6 Spread or pipe the frosting on top of each cooled cupcake, leaving a well in the center of the frosting on each one. Dollop 1 tablespoon of the lemon curd into each well.

7 Store in an airtight container in the refrigerator for up to 3 days.

Cream-Filled Chocolate Cupcakes

Makes
12 cupcakes

Hostess snack cakes have a certain level of nostalgia, but they've got nothing on homemade cupcakes. Nevertheless, my girls always beg for them at the store, so I set out to make a copycat that 1) actually tastes delicious (no plasticky ganache here—it's all smooth and silky), and 2) is something I feel good about them eating.

CUPCAKES

Nonstick cooking spray

¾ cup plus 2 tablespoons (105 grams) gluten-free 1:1 replacement flour blend

⅓ cup (35 grams) unsweetened cocoa powder

¾ teaspoon baking powder

¾ teaspoon baking soda

½ teaspoon kosher salt

1 cup (200 grams) granulated sugar

¼ cup (50 grams) neutral oil, such as avocado, sunflower, grapeseed, or canola oil

1 large egg

1 teaspoon pure vanilla extract

½ cup (115 grams) whole milk

½ cup (120 grams) hot water

FILLING

4 tablespoons (½ stick) unsalted butter, at room temperature

½ cup (55 grams) powdered sugar

1 cup (130 grams) Marshmallow Fluff

1 teaspoon pure vanilla extract

GANACHE

1½ cups (255 grams) semisweet chocolate chips

2 tablespoons unsalted butter, cut into small cubes

½ cup (115 grams) heavy cream

1 **Make the cupcakes:** Preheat the oven to 350°F. Spray a 12-cup muffin tin with cooking spray.

2 In a medium bowl, combine the flour, cocoa powder, baking powder, baking soda, and salt.

3 In the bowl of a stand mixer fitted with the paddle attachment or in a large bowl using a handheld mixer, combine the granulated sugar, oil, egg, and vanilla and beat on medium speed until combined. Add the dry ingredients in three additions, alternating with the milk, and beat until smooth. Add the hot water and beat until combined and smooth (the batter will be very thin).

4 Divide the batter evenly among the prepared muffin cups. Bake for about 20 minutes, until a toothpick inserted into the center comes out with just a few moist crumbs attached. Remove from the oven and let cool completely, about 1 hour.

5 **Make the filling:** In the bowl of stand mixer fitted with the paddle attachment or in a large bowl using a handheld mixer, beat the butter and powdered sugar on medium-high speed until light and fluffy, about 2 minutes. Beat in the Fluff and vanilla until combined, about 1 minute.

Recipe continues

6 **Make the ganache:** Place the chocolate chips and butter in a small heatproof bowl or a large glass measuring cup.

7 In a small saucepan, heat the cream over medium-high heat just until it comes to a boil. Pour the hot cream over the chocolate chips and butter in the bowl and let stand for 1 minute, then whisk until smooth.

8 Use a melon baller or a round ½-tablespoon measuring spoon to scoop out a bit of the center of each cooled cupcake, making a well; reserve the cake you scoop out. Fill the wells with the cream filling, then replace the cake you removed, covering the cream and pressing the cake so it adheres. Transfer the remaining filling to a piping bag fitted with a small round tip (or to a plastic zip-top bag with the tip of one corner snipped off to create a small hole). Spread a layer of ganache on top of each cupcake. Pipe a squiggle of icing on top of the ganache on each cupcake. Refrigerate until set before serving, about 30 minutes.

9 Store in an airtight container in the refrigerator for up to 3 days.

Crème Brûlée Cupcakes

Makes
12 cupcakes

Crème brûlée is one of my all-time favorite desserts to order when I'm out to dinner, but if there is a piece of cake on the menu, I find choosing between the two to be impossible. That's why I had to pair them for the ultimate winner. If you don't have a kitchen torch, let this recipe be your sign to go get one (or you can use your broiler, but that's not nearly as fun).

CUPCAKES

1½ cups (205 grams) gluten-free 1:1 replacement flour blend

1½ teaspoons baking powder

½ teaspoon kosher salt

3 tablespoons unsalted butter, at room temperature

3 tablespoons neutral oil, such as avocado, sunflower, grapeseed, or canola oil

½ cup (100 grams) granulated sugar

½ cup packed (105 grams) dark brown sugar

2 large eggs

1 teaspoon pure vanilla extract

⅓ cup (75 grams) whole milk

TOPPING

2 large egg yolks

¼ cup (50 grams) granulated sugar

2 tablespoons cornstarch

1 cup (225 grams) whole milk

1 tablespoon unsalted butter

1 teaspoon pure vanilla extract

¼ cup (45 grams) turbinado sugar

1 **Make the cupcakes:** Preheat the oven to 350°F. Line a 12-cup muffin tin with cupcake liners.

2 In a medium bowl, combine the flour, baking powder, and salt.

3 In the bowl of a stand mixer fitted with the paddle attachment or in a large bowl using a handheld mixer, combine the butter, oil, granulated sugar, and brown sugar and beat on medium speed until fluffy, about 2 minutes. Add the eggs one at a time, beating until smooth after each addition. Beat in the vanilla. Add the dry ingredients in three additions, alternating with the milk, and beat until smooth, about 30 seconds.

4 Divide the batter evenly among the prepared muffin cups. Bake for about 20 minutes, until a toothpick inserted into the center comes out with just a few moist crumbs attached. Remove from the oven and transfer to a wire rack to cool completely, about 1 hour.

5 **Meanwhile, make the topping:** In a large heatproof bowl, whisk together the egg yolks, granulated sugar, and cornstarch until smooth.

6 In a small saucepan, heat the milk over medium-high heat until just boiling. While whisking continuously, slowly pour the hot milk into the egg yolk mixture and whisk until combined. Return the mixture to the saucepan and cook over medium heat until thick enough to coat the back of a spoon, about 2 minutes. Remove from the heat and whisk in the butter and vanilla. Refrigerate the custard until cool, about 1 hour.

Recipe continues

7 Pipe or spread the custard on top of each cooled cupcake, then freeze until firm, about 1 hour.

8 If not serving immediately, store the cupcakes in an airtight container in the refrigerator for up to 3 days. Top with the turbinado sugar and brûlée just before serving.

9 Sprinkle the tops with the turbinado sugar and brûlée with a kitchen torch until the sugar is melted and browned. (Alternatively, broil on high for about 2 minutes, until the sugar is melted and browned.) Let cool slightly before serving.

White Cake Cupcakes

Makes
12 cupcakes

The main difference between white cake and yellow cake is simply egg yolks. Leaving them out not only affects the color, it also makes these cupcakes ultra light and fluffy.

CUPCAKES

- 1½ cups (205 grams) gluten-free 1:1 replacement flour blend
- 1½ teaspoons baking powder
- ½ teaspoon kosher salt
- 3 tablespoons unsalted butter, at room temperature
- 3 tablespoons neutral oil, such as avocado, sunflower, grapeseed, or canola oil
- 1 cup (200 grams) granulated sugar
- 3 large egg whites
- 1 teaspoon pure vanilla extract
- ½ cup (115 grams) whole milk

FROSTING

- 1 cup (2 sticks) unsalted butter, at room temperature
- 4 cups (455 grams) powdered sugar
- 1 tablespoon whole milk
- 1 teaspoon pure vanilla extract
- 1 cup rainbow nonpareils, for decorating

1 **Make the cupcakes:** Preheat the oven to 350°F. Line a 12-cup muffin tin with cupcake liners.

2 In a medium bowl, combine the flour, baking powder, and salt.

3 In the bowl of a stand mixer fitted with the paddle attachment or in a large bowl using a handheld mixer, combine the butter, oil, and granulated sugar and beat on medium speed until fluffy, about 2 minutes. Add the egg whites one at a time, beating until smooth after each addition. Beat in the vanilla. Add the dry ingredients in three additions, alternating with the milk, and beat until smooth, about 30 seconds.

4 Divide the batter evenly among the prepared muffin cups. Bake for about 20 minutes, until a toothpick inserted into the center comes out with just a few moist crumbs attached. Remove from the oven and transfer to a wire rack to cool completely, about 1 hour.

5 **Meanwhile, make the frosting:** In the bowl of a stand mixer fitted with the whisk attachment or in a large bowl using a handheld mixer, combine the butter, powdered sugar, milk, and vanilla and beat on medium speed until combined. Scrape down the sides of the bowl and beat on high until light and fluffy, 2 to 5 minutes.

6 Spread or pipe the frosting on top of the cooled cupcakes. Place the nonpareils in shallow bowl. Gently dip and roll the top of each cupcake in the nonpareils to coat the surface. Do not press too hard or you will flatten the frosting! Store in an airtight container in the refrigerator for up to 3 days.

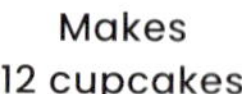

Chocolate Zucchini Cupcakes

Makes
12 cupcakes

These decadent cupcakes are the perfect way to sneak some veggies into my kids' day. It makes the cake super moist without introducing any unwanted earthy flavors, thanks to the rich chocolate taste.

CUPCAKES

1 cup (140 grams) gluten-free 1:1 replacement flour blend

½ cup (50 grams) unsweetened cocoa powder

1½ teaspoons baking powder

½ teaspoon kosher salt

6 tablespoons (¾ stick) unsalted butter, at room temperature

1 cup (200 grams) granulated sugar

2 large eggs

1 teaspoon pure vanilla extract

1 medium zucchini (1 pound), shredded (about 1½ cups) and squeezed to remove excess moisture

⅓ cup (75 grams) whole milk

FROSTING

½ cup (1 stick) unsalted butter, melted

⅔ cup (65 grams) unsweetened cocoa powder

3 cups (340 grams) powdered sugar

⅓ cup (75 grams) whole milk

1 teaspoon pure vanilla extract

1 **Make the cupcakes:** Preheat the oven to 350°F. Line a 12-cup muffin tin with cupcake liners.

2 In a medium bowl, whisk together the flour, cocoa powder, baking powder, and salt.

3 In the bowl of a stand mixer fitted with the whisk attachment or in a large bowl using a handheld mixer, beat the butter and granulated sugar on medium speed until light and fluffy, about 2 minutes. Add the eggs one at a time, beating until smooth after each addition. Beat in the vanilla. Stir in the zucchini. Add the dry ingredients in three additions, alternating with the milk, and beat until combined.

4 Divide the batter evenly among the prepared muffin cups. Bake for about 25 minutes, until a toothpick inserted into the center comes out with just a few moist crumbs attached. Remove from the oven and let cool in the muffin tin until cool enough to handle, then transfer to a wire rack to cool completely, about 1 hour.

5 **Meanwhile, make the frosting:** In the bowl of a stand mixer fitted with the whisk attachment or in a large bowl using a handheld mixer, combine the melted butter, cocoa powder, powdered sugar, milk, and vanilla and beat on medium speed until combined. Scrape down the sides of the bowl and beat on high until light and fluffy, 2 to 5 minutes.

6 Top the cooled cupcakes with the frosting. Store in an airtight container in the refrigerator for up to 3 days.

Cannoli Cones

Makes
12 cones

You'll have a little of the sweet ricotta cannoli cream (yep, the same one that's usually stuffed inside a cannoli) left over after making these cones—but it's so delicious, you won't mind! Keep it in an airtight container in your fridge for up to three days to enjoy atop a bowl of fruit, on waffles, or even just slathered on a piece of toast.

---

1 (16-ounce) container whole-milk ricotta

CONES

12 gluten-free sugar cones

1 cup (140 grams) gluten-free 1:1 replacement flour blend

1 teaspoon baking powder

¼ teaspoon kosher salt

2 tablespoons unsalted butter, at room temperature

2 tablespoons neutral oil, such as avocado, sunflower, grapeseed, or canola oil

⅔ cup (130 grams) granulated sugar

2 large egg whites

½ teaspoon pure vanilla extract

⅓ cup (75 grams) whole milk

CREAM

¾ cup (85 grams) powdered sugar

1 teaspoon pure vanilla extract

½ teaspoon lemon zest

Pinch of kosher salt

½ cup (90 grams) mini chocolate chips

1 Set a fine-mesh sieve over a medium bowl. Place the ricotta in the sieve and let drain in the refrigerator for at least 8 hours or up to 24 hours.

2 **Make the cones:** Preheat the oven to 350°F. Place the cones upright in silicone pop molds set on a rimmed baking sheet.

3 In a medium bowl, combine the flour, baking powder, and salt.

4 In the bowl of a stand mixer fitted with the paddle attachment or in a large bowl using a handheld mixer, combine the butter, oil, and granulated sugar and beat on medium speed until fluffy, about 2 minutes. Add the egg whites one at a time, beating until smooth after each addition. Beat in the vanilla. Add the dry ingredients, alternating with the milk, and beat until smooth, about 30 seconds.

5 Divide the batter evenly among the prepared cones. Bake for about 20 minutes, until a toothpick inserted into the center comes out with just a few moist crumbs attached. Carefully remove the cones from the molds and lay them down on the baking sheet. Bake for about 10 minutes more, until the cones are crisp. Remove from the oven and let cool completely, about 1 hour.

6 **Meanwhile, make the cream:** In a large bowl, whisk together the ricotta, powdered sugar, vanilla, lemon zest, and salt until smooth.

7 Use a metal or glass straw to poke a hole down through the center of the cake in each cone. Pipe the cream into the cones and on top of them. Dip the cones in the mini chocolate chips to cover the top layer of the cream.

8 These are best served the day they are made so the cones don't get soft, but you can store them in an airtight container in the rerigerator for up to 2 days.

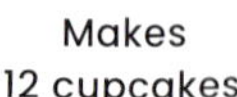

Sweet Potato Cinnamon Cupcakes

Makes 12 cupcakes

I love the flavor and texture the mashed freshly baked sweet potato adds to these cupcakes. Roasting them helps caramelize the sugars, adding a bit of extra sweetness, too, but if you're looking for a shortcut, swap in canned sweet potato or pumpkin puree.

CUPCAKES

1 large sweet potato (about 1 pound)

1¼ cups (175 grams) gluten-free 1:1 replacement flour blend

1½ teaspoons baking powder

1 teaspoon ground cinnamon

½ teaspoon kosher salt

6 tablespoons (¾ stick) unsalted butter, at room temperature

1 cup (200 grams) granulated sugar

2 large eggs

1 teaspoon pure vanilla extract

⅓ cup (75 grams) whole milk

FROSTING

½ cup (1 stick) unsalted butter, at room temperature

1 (8-ounce) block full-fat cream cheese, at room temperature

4 cups (455 grams) powdered sugar

1 tablespoon whole milk

1 teaspoon ground cinnamon

1 teaspoon pure vanilla extract

1 **Make the cupcakes:** Preheat the oven to 350°F. Line a 12-cup muffin tin with cupcake liners.

2 Wrap the sweet potato in aluminum foil and bake it directly on the oven rack for about 1 hour, until tender. Set aside until cool enough to handle.

3 Cut the sweet potato in half and scoop the flesh out of the skins into a food processor or blender. Puree until smooth.

4 In a medium bowl, combine the flour, baking powder, cinnamon, and salt.

5 In the bowl of a stand mixer fitted with the paddle attachment or in a large bowl using a handheld mixer, beat the butter and granulated sugar on medium speed until fluffy, about 2 minutes. Add the sweet potato puree and beat until smooth. Add the eggs one at a time, beating until smooth after each addition. Beat in the vanilla. Add the dry ingredients in three additions, alternating with the milk, and beat until smooth, about 30 seconds.

6 Divide the batter evenly among the prepared muffin cups. Bake for 25 to 30 minutes, until lightly golden on top. Remove from the oven and transfer to a wire rack to cool completely, about 1 hour.

7 **Meanwhile, make the frosting:** In the bowl of a stand mixer fitted with the whisk attachment or in a large bowl using a handheld mixer, combine the butter, cream cheese, powdered sugar, milk, and cinnamon and beat on medium speed until smooth. Scrape down the sides of the bowl and beat on high until light and fluffy, 2 to 5 minutes.

8 Spread or pipe the frosting on top of the cooled cupcakes. Store in an airtight container in the refrigerator for up to 3 days.

Boston Cream Cupcakes

Makes 12 cupcakes

I never understood why Boston cream pie is called a pie—it's really a cake, and making a cupcake version couldn't be easier. Just fill a standard sponge cake with pastry cream, top with chocolate ganache, and you're golden.

CUPCAKES

- 1½ cups (205 grams) gluten-free 1:1 replacement flour blend
- 1½ teaspoons baking powder
- ½ teaspoon kosher salt
- 3 tablespoons unsalted butter, at room temperature
- 3 tablespoons neutral oil, such as avocado, sunflower, grapeseed, or canola oil
- 1 cup (200 grams) sugar
- 2 large eggs
- 1 teaspoon pure vanilla extract
- ⅓ cup (75 grams) whole milk

FILLING

- 2 large egg yolks
- ¼ cup (50 grams) sugar
- 2 tablespoons cornstarch
- 1 cup (225 grams) whole milk
- 1 tablespoon unsalted butter
- 1 teaspoon pure vanilla extract

GANACHE

- 1½ cups (255 grams) semisweet chocolate chips
- 2 tablespoons unsalted butter, cut into small cubes
- ½ cup (115 grams) heavy cream

1 **Make the cupcakes:** Preheat the oven to 350°F. Line a 12-cup muffin tin with cupcake liners.

2 In a medium bowl, combine the flour, baking powder, and salt.

3 In the bowl of a stand mixer fitted with the paddle attachment or in a large bowl using a handheld mixer, combine the butter, oil, and sugar and beat on medium speed until fluffy, about 2 minutes. Add the eggs one at a time, beating until smooth after each addition. Beat in the vanilla. Add the dry ingredients in three additions, alternating with the milk, and beat until smooth, about 30 seconds.

4 Divide the batter evenly among the prepared muffin cups. Bake for about 20 minutes, until a toothpick inserted into the center comes out with just a few moist crumbs attached. Remove from the oven and transfer to a wire rack to cool completely, about 1 hour.

5 **Meanwhile, make the filling:** In a large heatproof bowl, whisk together the egg yolks, sugar, and cornstarch until smooth.

6 In a small saucepan, heat the milk over medium-high heat until just boiling. While whisking continuously, slowly pour the hot milk into the egg yolk mixture and whisk until combined. Return the mixture to the pan and cook over medium heat until thick enough to coat the back of a spoon, about 2 minutes. Remove from the heat and whisk in the butter

Recipe continues

and vanilla. Refrigerate the custard until cool, about 1 hour.

7 **Make the ganache:** Place the chocolate chips and butter in a small heatproof bowl or a large glass measuring cup.

8 In a small saucepan, heat the cream over medium-high heat just until it comes to a boil. Pour the hot cream over the chocolate chips and butter in the bowl and let stand for 1 minute, then whisk until smooth.

9 Use a melon baller or a round ½-tablespoon measuring spoon to scoop out a bit of the center of each cooled cupcake, making a well. Fill the wells with the custard, letting it overflow to create a layer on top, then spread a layer of ganache over the custard. Refrigerate until set before serving, about 30 minutes.

10 Store in an airtight container in the refrigerator for up to 3 days.

Millionaire's Cupcakes

Makes
12 cupcakes

Classic millionaire's bars have a layer of tender, crumbly shortbread topped with thick layers of caramel and chocolate ganache. I gave them a full makeover in this equally rich dessert. Rather than shortbread, the silky-smooth caramel and chocolate top moist, tender cupcakes.

CUPCAKES

1½ cups (205 grams) gluten-free 1:1 replacement flour blend

1½ teaspoons baking powder

½ teaspoon kosher salt

3 tablespoons unsalted butter, at room temperature

3 tablespoons neutral oil, such as avocado, sunflower, grapeseed, or canola oil

1 cup (200 grams) sugar

2 large eggs

1 teaspoon pure vanilla extract

⅓ cup (75 grams) whole milk

FROSTING

1½ cups (255 grams) semisweet chocolate chips

2 tablespoons unsalted butter, cut into small cubes

½ cup (115 grams) heavy cream

CARAMEL FILLING

1½ cups (300 grams) sugar

6 tablespoons (¾ stick) unsalted butter, cut into 1-tablespoon slices

⅓ cup (75 grams) heavy cream

1 **Make the cupcakes:** Preheat the oven to 350°F. Line a 12-cup muffin tin with cupcake liners.

2 In a medium bowl, combine the flour, baking powder, and salt.

3 In the bowl of a stand mixer fitted with the paddle attachment or in a large bowl using a handheld mixer, combine the butter, oil, and sugar and beat on medium speed until fluffy, about 2 minutes. Add the eggs one at a time, beating until smooth after each addition. Beat in the vanilla. Add the dry ingredients in three additions, alternating with the milk, and beat until smooth, about 30 seconds.

4 Divide the batter evenly among the prepared muffin cups. Bake for about 20 minutes, until a toothpick inserted into the center comes out with just a few moist crumbs attached. Remove from the oven and transfer to a wire rack to cool completely, about 1 hour.

5 **Meanwhile, make the frosting:** Place the chocolate chips and butter in the bowl of a stand mixer fitted with the whisk attachment or in a large bowl.

6 In a small saucepan, heat the cream over medium-high heat until boiling. Pour the boiling cream over the chocolate chips and let stand for 1 minute, then whisk until melted and smooth. Refrigerate until cool, about 1 hour.

Recipe continues

7 **Make the filling:** In a medium saucepan, combine the sugar and ⅓ cup (80 grams) water and heat over medium-high heat, stirring, until the sugar has dissolved. Continue to heat, without stirring, until the mixture turns amber, 5 to 10 minutes. Remove the pan from the heat and carefully whisk in the butter and cream until melted and combined. Set the caramel filling aside to cool.

8 When the frosting has cooled, affix the bowl to the stand mixer or use a handheld mixer and beat on medium-high speed until light and fluffy, 2 to 5 minutes.

9 Use a melon baller or a round ½-tablespoon measuring spoon to scoop out a bit of the center of each cooled cupcake, making a well. Fill the wells with the caramel filling, then spread or pipe the frosting on top of each one.

10 Store in an airtight container in the refrigerator for up to 3 days.

PIES

Stone Fruit Galette

Makes
one 10-inch galette;
serves 8 to 12

A layer of graham cracker crumbs between the crust and the fruit helps soak up extra juices, keeping your crust crisp while adding flavor. For an even flakier crust, use European butter (it's also my favorite for croissants, page 99), which has a higher fat content; you may need a touch less water in the dough.

- 1¼ cups (175 grams) gluten-free 1:1 replacement flour blend, plus more for dusting
- ½ cup (100 grams) plus 1 tablespoon granulated sugar
- ½ teaspoon kosher salt
- ½ cup (1 stick) cold unsalted butter, cut into small cubes
- 1½ teaspoons apple cider vinegar
- 4 to 5 tablespoons ice water
- 4 gluten-free graham crackers (65 grams)
- 2 pounds stone fruit, such as peaches, plums, nectarines, cherries and/or apricots, pitted and sliced (about 5 cups)
- ⅓ cup (40 grams) cornstarch
- 1 large egg, lightly beaten, for egg wash
- 1 tablespoon turbinado sugar

1 In a medium bowl, whisk together the flour, 1 tablespoon of the granulated sugar, and the salt. Add the butter and toss to coat with the flour mixture, then smush the butter into flat discs with your thumb and forefinger to grind it into the flour mixture. Sprinkle the vinegar over the flour-butter mixture and toss to coat. Sprinkle the ice water over the mixture 1 tablespoon at a time, stirring after each addition, until a shaggy dough forms.

2 Dump the dough out onto a clean work surface and lightly knead until it starts to hold together. Using a bench scraper, cut, stack, and press the dough (to avoid overworking the butter) until you have a smooth disc. Wrap tightly in plastic wrap and refrigerate for at least 1 hour or up to 8 hours.

3 Preheat the oven to 400°F. Line a baking sheet with parchment paper.

4 On a lightly floured surface, roll out the chilled dough to a roughly 13-inch round. Transfer the dough to the prepared baking sheet.

5 Place the graham crackers in a resealable plastic bag and smash with a rolling pin into fine crumbs. Spread the crumbs in a roughly 8-inch circle in the center of the dough. Refrigerate while you prepare the fruit.

6 In a large bowl, combine the stone fruit, remaining granulated sugar, and the cornstarch and toss to coat. (Alternatively, sort the fruit into bowls by color and divide the cornstarch and sugar among the bowls, then toss to combine.) Arrange the fruit on top of the graham cracker crumbs as desired. Fold the exposed dough up over the fruit, leaving the center uncovered and pleating the dough as needed as you work your way around the circle.

7 Brush the egg wash over the pleated edge of the dough and sprinkle it with the turbinado sugar. Bake for about 1 hour, until the crust is golden and the filling is bubbling. Let cool completely, about 1 hour, before slicing. Store, well wrapped, in the refrigerator for up to 3 days.

Sour Cherry Pie

Makes one 9-inch pie; serves 6 to 8

This homemade cherry pie is so much better than the goop you get in a can! Sour cherries have an incredibly short season, so make this at the height of summer when fresh ones are available, or opt for frozen. If you use frozen pitted cherries, start with 2½ pounds.

- 2½ cups (345 grams) gluten-free 1:1 replacement flour blend, plus more for dusting
- 1 cup (200 grams) plus 2 tablespoons granulated sugar
- 1 teaspoon kosher salt
- 1 cup (2 sticks) cold unsalted butter, cut into small cubes
- 1 tablespoon apple cider vinegar
- 8 to 12 tablespoons ice water
- 3 pounds pitted fresh sour cherries (see headnote), halved (about 7 cups)
- ⅓ cup (40 grams) cornstarch
- ½ teaspoon pure almond extract
- ½ teaspoon pure vanilla extract
- 1 large egg, lightly beaten, for egg wash
- 1 tablespoon turbinado sugar

1 In a medium bowl, whisk together the flour, 2 tablespoons of the granulated sugar, and the salt. Add the butter and toss to coat with the flour mixture, then smush the butter into flat discs with your thumb and forefinger to grind it into the flour mixture. Sprinkle the vinegar over the flour-butter mixture and toss to coat. Sprinkle the ice water over the mixture 1 tablespoon at a time, stirring after each addition, until a shaggy dough forms.

2 Dump the dough out onto a clean work surface and lightly knead until it starts to hold together. Using a bench scraper, cut, stack, and press the dough (to avoid overworking the butter) until you have a smooth disc. Divide the disc in half and form each half into a ball. Wrap each ball tightly in plastic wrap and refrigerate for at least 1 hour or up to 8 hours.

3 Preheat the oven to 400°F.

4 Place one of the dough balls on a lightly floured surface and roll it out to a roughly 12-inch round. Transfer it to a 9-inch pie plate, pressing the dough lightly against the bottom and sides of the pie plate. Roll the remaining dough out to a roughly 12-inch round. Using a pizza cutter, cut it into twelve 1-inch-wide strips.

5 Place the cherries in a large bowl and add the remaining 1 cup granulated sugar, the cornstarch, almond extract, and vanilla and toss to combine. Transfer the cherry mixture to the dough in the pie plate and arrange the strips of dough in a lattice pattern over the top. Fold the edges of the lattice strips under the edge of the bottom dough and crimp to seal.

6 Brush the egg wash over the lattice and sprinkle with the turbinado sugar. Bake for about 1 hour, until the crust is golden and the filling is bubbling. Remove from the oven and transfer to a wire rack to cool completely before slicing, about 2 hours.

7 Store, covered, in the refrigerator for up to 4 days.

Frangipane Fruit Tart

Makes
one 9-inch tart;
serves 12 to 16

I developed this almond-cream-based tart to work with any fruit. Use colorful berries in the spring and summer, then swap in sliced apples or pears in the fall and winter to enjoy this recipe all year long.

CRUST

- 1¼ cups (175 grams) gluten-free 1:1 replacement flour blend
- ½ cup (100 grams) sugar
- ½ teaspoon kosher salt
- ½ cup (1 stick) cold unsalted butter, cut into small cubes
- 1 large egg

FILLING

- ½ cup (1 stick) unsalted butter, at room temperature
- ½ cup (100 grams) sugar
- 2 large eggs
- 2 teaspoons pure vanilla extract
- 1 teaspoon pure almond extract
- 1 cup (95 grams) almond flour
- ¼ teaspoon kosher salt
- 2 cups fruit, such as berries or thinly sliced apples

1 **Make the crust:** Preheat the oven to 400°F.

2 In a large bowl, whisk together the flour, sugar, and salt. Add the butter and work it into the flour mixture using your hands until the mixture has a coarse breadcrumb texture. Stir in the egg until a shaggy dough forms, then knead until a smooth dough forms.

3 Roll the dough out to a 10-inch round. Press the dough round over the bottom and up the sides of a 9-inch tart pan with a removable bottom. Trim any excess dough. Dock the dough all over with a fork. Bake for about 15 minutes, until golden. Remove from the oven and let cool for about 15 minutes. Reduce the oven temperature to 350°F.

4 **Make the filling:** In a large bowl, beat the butter and sugar with a handheld mixer on medium speed until light and fluffy, about 2 minutes. Beat in the eggs one at a time. Beat in the vanilla and almond extract, then add the almond flour and salt and beat until smooth.

5 Pour the filling into the cooled tart shell. Nestle the fruit into the filling. Bake for 30 to 35 minutes, until golden on top. Remove from the oven and let cool completely before slicing, about 1 hour. Store, covered, in the refrigerator for up to 2 days.

Chocolate Fluffernutter Pie

Makes one 9-inch pie; serves 8 to 12

This one is for all of you who put Fluff in your peanut butter sandwiches and peanut butter on your Oreos as a kid. You can leave it as is, or add extra flair by topping with chopped Oreos, peanut butter cups, drizzles of peanut butter, and/or chocolate syrup.

CRUST

- 20 gluten-free chocolate sandwich cookies, such as gluten-free Oreos (225 grams)
- 4 tablespoons (½ stick) unsalted butter, melted

FILLING

- 1 (8-ounce) block full-fat cream cheese, at room temperature
- 1 cup (255 grams) creamy peanut butter
- 1 (7-ounce) container Marshmallow Fluff
- ½ cup (55 grams) powdered sugar
- 1 teaspoon pure vanilla extract
- 2 cups (455 grams) heavy cream

1 **Make the crust:** Preheat the oven to 350°F.

2 In a food processor, pulse the Oreos until finely ground. With the motor running, drizzle in the melted butter until the Oreo crumbs start to clump together. Press the mixture into an even layer in a 9-inch pie plate. Line the crust with a piece of parchment paper and fill with pie weights or dried beans. Bake for about 15 minutes, until set. Remove from the oven and carefully remove the pie weights or beans. Let cool completely, about 20 minutes.

3 **Make the filling:** In the bowl of a stand mixer fitted with the paddle attachment, combine the cream cheese, peanut butter, half the Fluff, the powdered sugar, and the vanilla and beat on medium speed until combined, about 1 minute.

4 Transfer the mixture to a separate bowl and clean the stand mixer bowl. Return the bowl to the mixer and, using the whisk attachment, beat the cream until medium peaks form, about 3 minutes. Transfer half the whipped cream to the bowl with the peanut butter mixture and fold them together until completely combined. Add the remaining Fluff to the mixer bowl with the remaining whipped cream and beat on high until combined and fluffy, about 1 minute.

5 Spread the peanut butter mixture over the cooled crust, then top with the Fluff mixture and refrigerate until set before serving, at least 4 hours. Store, covered, in the refrigerator for up to 3 days.

Coconut Caramel Chocolate Pie

Makes one 9-inch pie; serves 12 to 16

Samoas (also known as Caramel deLites) are my favorite Girl Scout cookie. Here I reinvisioned the cookie's flavors—caramel, coconut, and chocolate—into a pie with a macaroon crust that couldn't be easier to make.

CRUST

- Nonstick cooking spray
- 2 large egg whites
- ½ cup (100 grams) sugar
- 1 teaspoon pure vanilla extract
- Pinch of kosher salt
- 2½ cups (210 grams) unsweetened shredded coconut

CARAMEL FILLING

- 1½ cups (300 grams) sugar
- 6 tablespoons (¾ stick) unsalted butter
- ⅓ cup (75 grams) heavy cream

GANACHE

- 1½ cups (255 grams) semisweet chocolate chips
- 2 tablespoons unsalted butter, cubed
- ½ cup (115 grams) heavy cream
- Flaky sea salt, for garnish

1 **Make the crust:** Preheat the oven to 350°F. Coat a 9-inch pie plate with cooking spray.

2 In the bowl of a stand mixer fitted with the whisk attachment or in a large bowl using a handheld mixer, beat the egg whites on medium-high speed until medium peaks form, about 4 minutes. Gradually add the sugar and beat until stiff peaks form, about 3 minutes. Beat in the vanilla and salt. Fold in the coconut.

3 Press the coconut mixture over the bottom and up the sides of the prepared pie plate, then spray with cooking spray. Line the crust with parchment paper and fill it with pie weights or dried beans. Bake for about 20 minutes, until the edges of the crust start to turn golden. Carefully remove the parchment and pie weights or beans and bake for about 10 minutes more, until golden. Remove from the oven and let cool completely, about 20 minutes.

4 **Make the caramel filling:** In a medium saucepan, combine the sugar and ⅓ cup (80 grams) water and heat over medium-high heat, stirring, until the sugar has dissolved. Continue to cook, without stirring, until the mixture turns amber, 5 to 10 minutes. Remove the pan from the heat and carefully whisk in the butter and cream. Pour the caramel into the cooled crust and refrigerate until set, about 30 minutes.

5 **Make the ganache:** Place the chocolate chips and butter in a small heatproof bowl.

6 In a small saucepan, heat the cream over medium-high heat just until it comes to a boil. Pour the hot cream over the chocolate chips and butter in the bowl and let stand for 1 minute, then whisk until smooth. Spread the ganache over the caramel, then sprinkle with flaky salt. Refrigerate until the ganache hardens before serving, about 30 minutes.

7 Store, wrapped, in the refrigerator for up to 3 days.

Red Wine Pear Tart

Makes one 10-inch tart; serves 8 to 12

Preparing this wine-soaked tart upside down, just like a tarte tatin, ensures the crust gets super crispy. No soggy bottoms here! If any of the pears stick to the pan when you invert it, don't fret. Use a spatula to transfer them from the skillet back to the top of the tart. Serve this one with a large dollop of freshly whipped cream.

DOUGH

- 1¼ cups (175 grams) gluten-free 1:1 replacement flour blend
- 1 tablespoon sugar
- ½ teaspoon kosher salt
- ½ cup (1 stick) cold unsalted butter, cut into small cubes
- 1½ teaspoons apple cider vinegar
- 4 to 5 tablespoons ice water

FILLING

- ½ cup (100 grams) sugar
- ½ cup (1 stick) unsalted butter, thinly sliced
- 5 medium pears, peeled, stemmed, halved, and cored
- ½ cup pinot noir

1 **Make the dough:** In a medium bowl, whisk together the flour, sugar, and salt. Add the butter and toss to coat with the flour mixture, then smush the butter into flat discs with your thumb and forefinger to grind it into the flour mixture. Sprinkle the vinegar over the flour-butter mixture and toss to coat. Sprinkle the ice water over the mixture 1 tablespoon at a time, stirring after each addition, until a shaggy dough forms.

2 Dump the dough out onto a clean work surface and lightly knead until it starts to hold together. Using a bench scraper, cut, stack, and press the dough (to avoid overworking the butter) until you have a smooth disc. Wrap tightly in plastic wrap and refrigerate for at least 1 hour or up to 8 hours.

3 **Make the filling:** Spread the sugar over the bottom of a large enameled cast-iron or oven-safe nonstick skillet, then top it with the butter slices. Arrange the pears over the butter, cut-side down, then drizzle with the wine. Bring the mixture to a simmer over medium-high heat, then reduce the heat to maintain a simmer and cook, basting the pears with the liquid often, until the pears are tender and the juices have thickened, about 45 minutes.

4 Preheat the oven to 400°F.

5 Roll the dough out to a roughly 12-inch round and transfer it to a baking sheet. Refrigerate until firm, about 15 minutes. Quickly slide the dough round off the baking sheet and over the top of the skillet and then carefully tuck the edges of the dough into the pan. Bake for about 25 minutes, until the crust is golden. Remove from the oven and let cool slightly, about 20 minutes, then invert onto a plate and serve. This is best eaten the day it's made, but it can be stored, covered, in the refrigerator for up to 2 days.

Lemon Poppy Seed Tart

Makes one 9-inch tart; serves 12 to 16

I've always been a fan of lemon meringue pie, but this tart takes it to the next level with poppy seeds dotting the crust. It's filled with my favorite lemon curd (a recipe you can use in other recipes, like the Lemon Cupcakes on page 137).

CRUST

1¼ cups (175 grams) gluten-free 1:1 replacement flour blend

½ cup (100 grams) granulated sugar

½ teaspoon kosher salt

½ cup (1 stick) cold unsalted butter, cut into small cubes

1 large egg

1 tablespoon poppy seeds

LEMON CURD

6 large egg yolks (save the whites for the meringue)

1 cup (200 grams) sugar

2 tablespoons lemon zest

½ cup (120 grams) fresh lemon juice

Pinch of kosher salt

½ cup (1 stick) unsalted butter, thinly sliced

MERINGUE

3 large egg whites

¼ teaspoon cream of tartar

Pinch of kosher salt

⅓ cup (65 grams) sugar

½ teaspoon pure vanilla extract

1 **Make the crust:** Preheat the oven to 400°F.

2 In a large bowl, whisk together the flour, sugar, and salt. Add the butter and work it into the flour mixture using your hands until the mixture has a coarse breadcrumb texture. Stir in the egg and the poppy seeds until a shaggy dough forms, then knead until the dough is smooth.

3 Roll the dough out to a 10-inch round. Press the dough over the bottom and up the sides of a 9-inch tart pan with a removable bottom. Trim any excess dough. Dock the dough all over with a fork. Line the dough with parchment paper and fill it with pie weights or dried beans. Bake for 15 minutes, then carefully remove the parchment paper and pie weights or beans and bake for about 10 minutes more, until golden. Remove from the oven and let cool completely, about 20 minutes.

4 **Make the lemon curd:** Fill a large saucepan with 1 to 2 inches of water. Bring to a boil over high heat.

5 In a large heatproof bowl, whisk together the egg yolks, sugar, lemon zest, lemon juice, and salt until smooth. Set the bowl over the boiling water and cook, whisking continuously, until the mixture is thick enough to coat the back of a spoon, about 15 minutes. Remove the bowl from the heat and whisk in the butter one piece at a time until emulsified. Spread the lemon curd over the cooled crust. Refrigerate until set, about 2 hours.

6 **Make the meringue:** In the bowl of a stand mixer fitted with the whisk attachment or in a large bowl using a handheld mixer, combine the egg whites, cream of tartar, and salt and beat on medium speed until soft peaks form, about 2 minutes. With the mixer running, gradually add the sugar and beat until stiff, glossy peaks form, about 4 minutes more. Beat in the vanilla.

7 Arrange the meringue on top of the cooled lemon curd. Using a kitchen torch, lightly toast the meringue. (Alternatively, place the tart under the broiler, rotating to toast evenly, about 2 minutes.) Serve immediately.

Apple & Brie Galette

Makes one 10-inch galette; serves 8 to 12

I have to admit, sometimes (*sometimes*) I pass on dessert for a good cheese plate instead. This recipe is the best of both worlds: a little sweet, a little savory, and 100% satisfying. The drizzle of honey on top adds just a touch more sweetness, but if you really want to take it up a notch try it with hot honey for a little heat.

- 1¼ cups (175 grams) gluten-free 1:1 replacement flour blend, plus more for dusting
- ½ cup (100 grams) plus 1 tablespoon sugar
- ½ teaspoon kosher salt
- ½ cup (1 stick) cold unsalted butter, cut into small cubes
- 1½ teaspoons apple cider vinegar
- 4 to 5 tablespoons ice water
- 8 ounces Brie cheese, rind removed and thinly sliced
- 1½ pounds sweet apples, such as Honeycrisp, Fuji, and/or Gala, cored and sliced (about 5 cups)
- ⅓ cup (40 grams) cornstarch
- 2 tablespoons fresh lemon juice
- 1 large egg, lightly beaten, for egg wash
- Honey, for serving

1 In a medium bowl, whisk together the flour, 1 tablespoon of the sugar, and salt. Add the butter and toss to coat with the flour mixture, then smush the butter into flat discs with your thumb and forefinger to grind it into the flour mixture. Sprinkle the vinegar over the flour-butter mixture and toss to coat. Sprinkle the ice water over the mixture 1 tablespoon at a time, stirring after each addition, until a shaggy dough forms.

2 Dump the dough out onto a clean work surface and lightly knead until it starts to hold together. Using a bench scraper, cut, stack, and press the dough (to avoid overworking the butter) until you have a smooth disc. Wrap tightly in plastic wrap and refrigerate for at least 1 hour or up to 8 hours.

3 Preheat the oven to 400°F. Line a baking sheet with parchment paper.

4 On a lightly floured surface, roll the dough out to a roughly 13-inch round. Transfer the dough to the prepared baking sheet. Place the Brie slices in a roughly 8-inch circle in the center of the dough.

5 In a large bowl, combine the apples, remaining ½ cup (100 grams) sugar, the cornstarch, and the lemon juice and toss to coat. Arrange the apples on top of the Brie (I like to fan the apple slices out to create a flower shape). Fold the exposed dough up over the fruit, leaving the center uncovered and pleating the dough as needed as you work your way around the circle.

6 Brush the egg wash over the pleated edge of the dough. Bake for about 1 hour, until the crust is golden and the filling is bubbling. Remove from the oven and let cool completely before slicing, about 1 hour.

7 Just before serving, drizzle with honey. Store leftovers, well wrapped, in the refrigerator for up to 3 days.

Skillet Blueberry Crumble

Makes one 10- to 12-inch crumble; serves 10 to 12

I love making this in the summer after a day of picking blueberries with my girls, but it also works with any fruit you have a whole bunch of. Try it with other berries, pitted cherries, or even sliced peaches, apples, or pears.

- Nonstick cooking spray
- 6 cups (1,140 grams) blueberries
- ½ cup (100 grams) granulated sugar
- ¼ cup (30 grams) cornstarch
- Zest and juice of 1 lemon
- 1 teaspoon pure vanilla extract
- 1 teaspoon kosher salt
- 1 cup (140 grams) gluten-free 1:1 replacement flour blend
- 1 cup (125 grams) gluten-free rolled oats
- ½ cup packed (105 grams) light brown sugar
- ½ cup (1 stick) unsalted butter, melted

1 Preheat the oven to 400°F. Spray a 10- to 12-inch cast-iron skillet with cooking spray.

2 In the skillet, combine the blueberries, granulated sugar, cornstarch, lemon juice, vanilla, and ½ teaspoon of the salt and toss to coat.

3 In a medium bowl, combine the flour, oats, brown sugar, lemon zest, and remaining ½ teaspoon salt. Add the melted butter and stir until the mixture begins to clump together. Evenly sprinkle the oat mixture over the blueberries in the skillet.

4 Bake for about 45 minutes, until the crumble is golden and the blueberries are bubbling. Let cool slightly before serving, or let cool completely and store in an airtight container in the refrigerator for up to 3 days.

Grandma Doris's Apple Pie

Makes one 9-inch pie; serves 6 to 8

I took my grandma Doris's apple pie recipe and gave it just the slightest flavor update with some vanilla bean paste and ground cardamom. My perfect apple pie includes a mix of apples—a few McIntoshes, which break down into a melt-in-your-mouth texture, plus some Granny Smiths, which hold their shape while adding tartness. But feel free to use any combination of your favorite apples.

- 2½ cups (350 grams) gluten-free 1:1 replacement flour blend, plus more for dusting
- 1 cup (200 grams) plus 2 tablespoons granulated sugar
- 1 teaspoon kosher salt
- 1 cup (2 sticks) cold unsalted butter, cut into small cubes
- 1 tablespoon apple cider vinegar
- 8 to 12 tablespoons ice water
- 3 pounds apples, peeled, cored, and thinly sliced (about 7 cups)
- ⅓ cup (40 grams) cornstarch
- 1 tablespoon vanilla bean paste
- 1 teaspoon ground cinnamon
- ½ teaspoon ground cardamom
- 1 large egg, lightly beaten, for egg wash
- 1 tablespoon turbinado sugar

1 In a medium bowl, whisk together the flour, 2 tablespoons of the granulated sugar, and the salt. Add the butter and toss to coat with the flour mixture, then smush the butter into flat discs with your thumb and forefinger to grind it into the flour mixture. Sprinkle the vinegar over the flour-butter mixture and toss to coat. Sprinkle the ice water over the mixture 1 tablespoon at a time, stirring after each addition, until the dough begins to hold together.

2 Dump the dough out onto a clean work surface and very lightly knead until it starts to hold together. Form the dough into a ball and cut the ball in half. Transfer each ball to a piece of plastic wrap, smush the dough into a disc, wrap tightly, and refrigerate until firm, about 30 minutes.

3 Place one disc of dough on a lightly floured surface and roll it out to a roughly 6×12-inch rectangle. With one short end facing you, fold the bottom third up and the upper third down, as if you were folding a letter. Rotate the dough 90 degrees and repeat the rolling and letterfold. Wrap tightly in plastic wrap and refrigerate until firm, about 30 minutes. Repeat with the remaining dough ball.

4 Preheat the oven to 400°F.

5 Place one of the dough balls on a lightly floured surface and roll it out to a roughly 12-inch round. Transfer it to a 9-inch pie plate, pressing the dough lightly against the bottom and sides of the pie plate. Roll the remaining dough out to a

Recipe continues

roughly 12-inch round. Using a pizza cutter, cut it into six 2-inch-wide strips.

6 Place the apples in a large bowl, add the remaining 1 cup (200 grams) granulated sugar, the cornstarch, vanilla, cinnamon, and cardamom, and toss to coat. Transfer the apple mixture to the dough in the pie plate and arrange the strips of dough in a lattice pattern over the top. Fold the edges of the lattice strips under the edge of the bottom dough and crimp to seal.

7 Brush the egg wash over the crust and sprinkle with the turbinado sugar. Bake for about 1 hour, until the crust is golden and the filling is bubbling. Remove from the oven and transfer to a wire rack to cool completely before slicing and serving, about 2 hours.

8 Store leftovers, covered, in the refrigerator for up to 4 days.

Chocolate Pecan Pie

Makes one 9-inch pie; serves 6 to 8

At the East Pole, one of my go-to restaurants in NYC, I had a pie that changed my life. I don't mean to be dramatic, but after I had it, I really couldn't stop thinking about it, and I needed to re-create it at home. The rich flavors of pecan pie and chocolate ganache meld beautifully together all atop a flaky crust. It's the only Thanksgiving pie I'll ever need.

- 1¼ cups (175 grams) gluten-free 1:1 replacement flour blend, plus more for dusting
- 1 tablespoon granulated sugar
- ½ teaspoon kosher salt
- ½ cup (1 stick) cold unsalted butter, cut into small cubes, plus 4 tablespoons (½ stick) unsalted butter, melted
- 1½ teaspoons apple cider vinegar
- 4 to 5 tablespoons ice water
- 1 cup (170 grams) dark chocolate chips
- ¾ cup (170 grams) heavy cream
- 3 large eggs
- ¾ cup packed (160 grams) dark brown sugar
- ¼ cup (80 grams) pure maple syrup
- 2 teaspoons pure vanilla extract
- ½ teaspoon kosher salt
- 2 cups (240 grams) pecan halves

1 In a medium bowl, combine the flour, granulated sugar, and salt. Add the cold butter and toss to coat with the flour mixture, then smush the butter into flat discs with your thumb and forefinger to grind it into the flour mixture. Sprinkle the vinegar over the flour-butter mixture and toss to coat. Sprinkle the ice water over the mixture 1 tablespoon at a time, stirring after each addition, until a shaggy dough forms.

2 Dump the dough out onto a clean work surface and lightly knead until it starts to hold together. Using a bench scraper, cut, stack, and press the dough (to avoid overworking the butter) until you have a smooth disc. Wrap tightly in plastic wrap and refrigerate for at least 1 hour or up to 8 hours.

3 Preheat the oven to 425°F.

4 Place the dough on a lightly floured surface and roll it out to a roughly 12-inch round. Transfer it to a 9-inch pie plate and press it lightly against the bottom and up the sides of the pie plate. Trim and crimp the edges and refrigerate until chilled, at least 15 minutes.

5 Dock the dough with a fork. Line the dough with parchment paper and fill it with pie weights or dried beans. Bake for about 10 minutes, until the edges of the crust are beginning to brown. Carefully remove the parchment paper and pie weights or beans and bake for about 5 minutes

Recipe continues

more, until the crust is golden. Remove from the oven and let cool completely, about 20 minutes. Reduce the oven temperature to 375°F.

6 Place chocolate chips in a heatproof medium bowl. In a small saucepan, bring ½ cup (115 grams) of the cream to a boil over medium-high heat. Pour the hot cream over the chocolate chips and let stand for 20 seconds, then stir until combined and thick. Pour the ganache into the cooled crust.

7 In a large bowl, whisk together the eggs, brown sugar, maple syrup, remaining ¼ cup (55 grams) cream, the melted butter, vanilla, and salt until smooth. Stir in the pecans. Scrape the mixture into the crust, spreading it into an even layer atop the ganache.

8 Place the pie plate on a rimmed baking sheet and bake for about 45 minutes, until the filling is set but still wobbles slightly. Remove from the oven and let cool completely before slicing, about 2 hours. Store leftovers, covered, in the refrigerator for up to 3 days.

ICE CREAM

Nutella Fudge Pops

Makes
12 to 15 pops

Inspired by no-churn ice cream, which simply calls for whipping together sweetened condensed milk and heavy cream before freezing into ice cream, these fudge pops simply use chocolate-hazelnut spread with cream for the same soft and creamy texture once frozen. To easily release the pops from the molds, dip the bottom of the molds in warm water for 10 to 20 seconds before pulling out the pops.

---

1 (13-ounce) jar chocolate-hazelnut spread, such as Nutella

2 cups (455 grams) heavy cream

1 cup sliced strawberries

1 In a large bowl, combine the chocolate-hazelnut spread and cream and beat with a handheld mixer on low speed until combined, then beat on high until soft peaks form, about 2 minutes.

2 Divide the cream mixture evenly among 12 to 15 pop molds. Slide the strawberries down the sides of the molds so they are pressed against the sides. Freeze until solid, at least 12 hours.

3 Wrap individually and store in an airtight container in the freezer for up to 3 months.

Cookies & Cream Ice Cream

Makes
5 cups

Using some corn syrup in addition to the granulated sugar makes this homemade ice cream extra creamy. Another trick for getting the creamiest ice cream at home? Freeze the container you plan to store the ice cream in so none of the ice cream melts when you transfer it from the ice cream machine to the container.

- 6 large egg yolks
- 2 cups (455 grams) heavy cream
- 1 cup (225 grams) whole milk
- ½ cup (100 grams) sugar
- 2 tablespoons light corn syrup
- Pinch of kosher salt
- 1 teaspoon pure vanilla extract
- 15 gluten-free chocolate sandwich cookies, such as gluten-free Oreos (170 grams), crushed into bite-size pieces

1 Place the egg yolks in a large heatproof bowl.

2 In a medium saucepan, whisk together the cream, milk, sugar, corn syrup, and salt. Bring to a simmer over medium-high heat, then remove from the heat. While whisking continuously, slowly pour the hot cream mixture into the egg yolks and whisk until combined. Strain the mixture through a fine-mesh sieve into an airtight container and stir in the vanilla. Cover with the lid and refrigerate the custard until very cold, at least 4 hours or up to 24 hours.

3 Churn the chilled custard in an ice cream machine following the manufacturer's instructions. Transfer the ice cream to an airtight container and stir in the cookie pieces, then cover with the lid and freeze until firm, about 4 hours. Store in the freezer for up to 3 months.

Banana Split Pudding Pops

Makes
10 to 12 pops

Banana pudding and banana splits combine in this dessert-on-a-stick masterpiece. Melt the chocolate chips in a tall glass (like a pint glass) and dip the pops directly into the glass to ensure you get as much chocolate as possible on each one.

- 2 cups (455 grams) whole milk
- ½ cup (100 grams) sugar
- 3 tablespoons cornstarch
- 1 teaspoon pure vanilla extract
- Pinch of kosher salt
- 3 very ripe bananas, mashed (about 1 cup)
- 1 cup (170 grams) milk chocolate chips
- 1 tablespoon coconut oil
- Sprinkles, chopped nuts, and/or crushed cookies, for topping

1 In a large saucepan, whisk together the milk, sugar, cornstarch, vanilla, and salt. Cook over medium-high heat, whisking often, until the mixture comes to a simmer and thickens, about 5 minutes. Remove from the heat and let cool to room temperature, about 1 hour, then whisk the mashed banana into the pudding. Divide the pudding among 10 to 12 ice pop molds and freeze until solid, at least 8 hours.

2 Line a baking sheet with parchment paper and place it in the freezer.

3 Place the chocolate chips and coconut oil in a tall microwave-safe glass or medium bowl and microwave in 30-second intervals, stirring after each, until melted and smooth.

4 Place your desired toppings in a shallow bowl. Working quickly, unmold one of the pops and dip it in the melted chocolate to coat, then roll it in the toppings. Place it on the prepared pan in the freezer and repeat to coat the remaining pops.

5 Store in an airtight container in the freezer for up to 1 month.

Red Velvet Ice Cream

Makes 4 cups

For the cake pieces in this recipe, make half the cake recipe (one layer) on page 51, but skip the frosting—this ice cream has a cream cheese swirl, so you still get that sweet-and-tangy combo. If making cake is too much, just skip it—you'll still get plenty of delicious red velvet flavor from the ice cream alone.

- 6 large egg yolks
- 2 cups (455 grams) heavy cream
- 1 cup (170 grams) buttermilk
- ¾ cup (150 grams) sugar
- 2 tablespoons light corn syrup
- Pinch of kosher salt
- 1 teaspoon pure vanilla extract
- 1 (8-ounce) block full-fat cream cheese, at room temperature
- 3 tablespoons unsweetened cocoa powder
- 5 drops red gel food coloring
- 2 cups cubed Red Velvet Cake (page 51; optional)

1 Place the egg yolks in a large heatproof bowl.

2 In a medium saucepan, whisk together the cream, buttermilk, ½ cup (100 grams) of the sugar, the corn syrup, and the salt. Bring to a simmer over medium-high heat, then remove from the heat. While whisking continuously, slowly pour the hot cream mixture into the egg yolks and whisk until combined. Strain the custard through a fine-mesh sieve into an airtight container and stir in the vanilla.

3 In a medium bowl, beat the cream cheese and remaining ¼ cup (50 grams) sugar with a handheld mixer on high speed until smooth. Gradually beat in ½ cup of the custard until smooth.

4 Whisk the cocoa powder and food coloring into the remaining custard (not the cream cheese mixture). Refrigerate the custard and the cream cheese mixture separately until very cold, at least 4 hours or up to 24 hours.

5 Churn the chilled custard in an ice cream machine following the manufacturer's instructions. Transfer the ice cream to an airtight container and fold in the cake cubes, then swirl in the cream cheese mixture. Cover with the lid and freeze until firm, about 4 hours. Store in the freezer for up to 3 months.

Pineapple Whip

Makes
2 cups

Just like you'd get at a theme park, but in the comfort of your own home! Top it off with some toasted flaked coconut, mini chocolate chips, maraschino cherries, or just good old sprinkles for extra fun. You can also serve this up in cones instead of dishes.

---

2 cups frozen pineapple

½ cup coconut cream

1 tablespoon honey

1 teaspoon fresh lime juice

Gluten-free ice cream cones, for serving (optional)

1 In a food processor, combine the pineapple, coconut cream, honey, and lime juice. Puree until smooth. Transfer to a piping bag fitted with a large star tip. If the mixture is too soft or liquidy, lay the piping bag down on a plate and place it in the freezer for about 20 minutes before serving.

2 Pipe the mixture into bowls or ice cream cones, if desired, and serve immediately.

VARIATIONS

STRAWBERRY WHIP

Replace 1 cup of the frozen pineapple with 1 cup frozen strawberries.

MANGO WHIP

Replace 1 cup of the frozen pineapple with 1 cup frozen cubed mango.

Rainbow Sherbet

Makes 4 cups

I've always loved sherbet—it's the perfect hybrid of sorbet and ice cream, colorful and fruity but so creamy from the dairy. I use gelatin in my recipe to ensure that it's nice and smooth—it helps the dairy mixture set up into just the right soft and bouncy texture without the need for an egg-based custard. I've also found it's the one setting agent that really prevents any ice crystals forming in the sherbet.

- 1 (¼-ounce) packet unflavored gelatin powder
- 2 cups (455 grams) whole milk
- 1 cup (225 grams) heavy cream
- ½ cup (100 grams) plus 1 tablespoon sugar
- 1 teaspoon pure vanilla extract
- 1 (6-ounce) container fresh raspberries
- ½ cup (120 grams) orange juice
- 1 drop orange gel food coloring
- ½ cup (120 grams) lime juice
- 1 drop green gel food coloring

1 In a large saucepan, stir together the gelatin and milk until the gelatin has dissolved. Add the cream, ½ cup (100 grams) of the sugar, and the vanilla and bring to a boil over medium-high heat, stirring until the sugar has dissolved. Remove from the heat and divide the mixture among 3 medium bowls.

2 In a blender, combine the raspberries and remaining 1 tablespoon sugar and blend until smooth. Strain the mixture into one of the bowls with the milk mixture and stir to combine. Stir the orange juice and orange food coloring into the second bowl of the milk mixture and the lime juice and the green food coloring into the final bowl of the milk mixture. Refrigerate all three bowls until the sherbet base is cold, at least 4 hours.

3 Working with one bowl at a time, churn each sherbet base in an ice cream machine until it has the consistency of soft serve, about 5 minutes. Transfer the churned mixture to an airtight container or a loaf pan and place it in the freezer while you churn the next sherbet base, then pour that into the container or pan over the first. Repeat with the final sherbet base, then gently swirl them together with a knife. Cover and freeze until firm, about 4 hours. Store in the freezer for up to 3 months.

Orange Sorbet

Makes
6 orange cups

Sorbet couldn't be easier to make, but what makes this recipe really special is the presentation. Hollow out the oranges and use the flesh to make the sorbet, then pile it back into the hollow orange halves for a beautiful bowl—no dishwashing required!

3 navel oranges (1½ pounds)

½ cup (100 grams) sugar

1 Cut a very thin slice off the top and bottom of each orange—just enough to make a flat surface so the hollowed halves will stand upright but not so much that you cut through the rind—then cut them in half crosswise. Scoop out the flesh, leaving the rinds intact, and transfer the flesh to a blender; set the rinds aside. Add the sugar and ¼ cup (60 grams) water to the blender and puree until smooth. Transfer the orange mixture to an ice cream machine and churn following the manufacturer's instructions.

2 Stand the hollow orange rinds upright on a baking sheet and divide the sorbet evenly among them. Freeze until firm, about 4 hours. Wrap individually in plastic wrap and freeze in an airtight container or zip-top bag for up to 3 months.

VARIATIONS

GRAPEFRUIT SORBET

Swap in 2 grapefruits for the 3 oranges and prepare the recipe as directed.

LEMON SORBET

Swap in 4 lemons for the 3 oranges, slicing them in half through the stem end instead of horizontally, and prepare the recipe as directed.

No-Churn Coffee Ice Cream

Makes 4 cups

A really good coffee ice cream doesn't require much—I use the cold-brew method to steep heavy cream with intense coffee flavor before whipping it up with sweetened condensed milk for the smoothest ice cream ever. If you like a more subtle coffee flavor, use spent grounds instead of fresh ones. It will mellow things out—plus, it's a great way to upcycle.

- **2½ cups (570 grams) heavy cream**
- **½ cup (40 grams) ground coffee**
- **1 (14-ounce) can sweetened condensed milk**
- **1 teaspoon pure vanilla extract**

1 In a large bowl, stir together the cream and the coffee. Cover and refrigerate overnight or for at least 8 hours.

2 Strain the cream mixture through a coffee filter into a clean large bowl; discard the coffee grounds. Add the condensed milk and vanilla and beat with a handheld mixer on high speed until soft peaks form, about 5 minutes. Transfer the mixture to an airtight container and smooth the top. Freeze until solid before serving, about 4 hours. Store in the freezer for up to 3 months.

Ice Cream Sandwiches

Makes
16 ice cream
sandwiches

I loved those classic stick-to-your-fingers ice cream sandwiches as a kid and knew I needed to come up with a gluten-free version to bring back that nostalgia. If you want to make these even easier, just spread a softened store-bought ice cream between the cookie layers instead of using the homemade no-churn ice cream in this recipe.

COOKIE LAYERS

Nonstick cooking spray

3 cups (415 grams) gluten-free 1:1 replacement flour blend

1 cup (100 grams) unsweetened cocoa powder

½ teaspoon kosher salt

1 cup (2 sticks) unsalted butter, at room temperature

1½ cups (300 grams) sugar

2 large eggs

2 teaspoons pure vanilla extract

NO-CHURN ICE CREAM

2½ cups (570 grams) heavy cream

1 (14-ounce) can sweetened condensed milk

1 teaspoon vanilla bean paste or pure vanilla extract

Sprinkles and/or mini chocolate chips (optional)

1 **Make the cookie layers:** Preheat the oven to 325°F. Line a 9×13-inch baking pan with parchment paper, leaving some overhang on the two long sides. Spray the parchment lightly with cooking spray.

2 In a medium bowl, whisk together the flour, cocoa powder, and salt.

3 In the bowl of a stand mixer fitted with the whisk attachment or in a large bowl using a handheld mixer, beat the butter and sugar on medium speed until smooth. Beat in the eggs one at a time. Beat in the vanilla. Stir the dry ingredients into the wet ingredients.

4 Press half the dough into an even layer in the prepared pan and, using a skewer, poke holes in even lines every 1 inch across the dough, creating a grid. Bake for about 10 minutes, until set. Remove from the oven and let cool in the pan until cool to the touch, about 20 minutes, then use the overhanging parchment to transfer to a wire rack to cool completely, about 30 minutes. Repeat with the remaining dough.

5 **Meanwhile, make the ice cream:** In a large bowl, combine the cream, condensed milk, and vanilla and beat with a handheld mixer on high speed until soft peaks form.

6 Line the baking pan with a fresh sheet of parchment, leaving some overhang on the two long sides. Place one of the cookie layers in the bottom of the pan, with the holes facing down. Spread the whipped cream mixture evenly over the top, then top with the other cookie layer, with the holes facing up. Freeze until solid, about 4 hours.

Recipe continues

7 Using the overhanging parchment, transfer the ice cream sandwich to a cutting board and cut into bars. Press the ice cream sides of each bar into sprinkles and/or mini chocolate chips, if desired.

8 Wrap individually and store in an airtight container in the freezer for up to 3 months.

VARIATIONS

RED VELVET ICE CREAM SANDWICHES

Omit the heavy cream, sweetened condensed milk, and vanilla bean paste. Prepare Red Velvet Ice Cream (page 192), but just after churning, spread the ice cream over the bottom cookie layer (instead of freezing it until solid). Top with the remaining cookie layer and continue with the recipe as directed.

COOKIES & CREAM ICE CREAM SANDWICHES

Omit the heavy cream, sweetened condensed milk, and vanilla bean paste. Prepare Cookies & Cream Ice Cream (page 188) , but just after churning, spread the ice cream over the bottom cookie layer (instead of freezing it until solid). Top with the remaining cookie layer and continue with the recipe as directed.

Brownie Batter Ice Cream

Makes 5 cups

I've been known to lick the bowl, beaters, and every other baking tool clean after making brownie batter, which inspired this recipe. The flavor truly is just like that, with chunks of brownies to boot.

BROWNIES

- Nonstick cooking spray
- 1 cup (140 grams) gluten-free 1:1 replacement flour blend
- ¾ cup (150 grams) sugar
- ½ cup (50 grams) unsweetened cocoa powder
- ½ teaspoon baking powder
- ½ teaspoon kosher salt
- 4 tablespoons (½ stick) unsalted butter, melted
- 1 large egg
- 2 tablespoons whole milk
- 1 teaspoon pure vanilla extract

ICE CREAM

- 6 large egg yolks
- 2 cups (455 grams) heavy cream
- 1 cup (225 grams) whole milk
- ¼ cup (50 grams) sugar
- 1 teaspoon pure vanilla extract

1 **Make the brownies:** Preheat the oven to 350°F. Line a loaf pan with parchment paper, leaving some overhang on the two long sides. Spray with cooking spray.

2 In a large bowl, whisk together the flour, sugar, cocoa powder, baking powder, and salt. Transfer 1 cup of the brownie mix to a small bowl and set aside for the ice cream.

3 Add the melted butter, egg, milk, and vanilla to the remaining flour mixture and whisk until a smooth batter forms. Pour the batter into the prepared pan and bake for 20 minutes, until the top is set and a toothpick inserted into the center comes out with just a few moist crumbs attached. Remove from the oven and let cool completely, about 1 hour.

4 Line a baking sheet with parchment paper. Remove the brownies from the pan and chop into bite-size pieces. Arrange in a single layer on the prepared pan and freeze until solid, at least 1 hour, or transfer to an airtight container and freeze for up to 3 months.

5 **Make the ice cream:** In a large heatproof bowl, whisk the egg yolks until smooth. Sprinkle the reserved 1 cup brownie mix on top.

6 In a medium saucepan, whisk together the cream, milk, and sugar. Bring to a simmer over medium-high heat. Remove from the heat. While whisking continuously, slowly pour the hot cream mixture into the egg yolk mixture and whisk until combined. Strain through a fine-mesh sieve into an airtight container, then stir in the vanilla. Cover and refrigerate the custard until very cold, at least 4 hours or up to 24 hours.

7 Churn the chilled custard in an ice cream machine following the manufacturer's instructions. Transfer the ice cream to an airtight container and stir in the brownie bites, then cover with the lid and freeze until firm, about 4 hours. Store in the freezer for up to 3 months.

Cookie Dough Ice Cream

Makes 5 cups

Finally! A cookie dough ice cream that's gluten-free. If you've ever stared longingly at the cookie-filled ice creams in the freezer aisle, this one is for you. I always make a double batch of the edible cookie dough bites to stash in the freezer. They're a delicious snack even without the ice cream.

COOKIE DOUGH

- 1 cup (140 grams) gluten-free 1:1 replacement flour blend
- ½ cup (1 stick) unsalted butter, melted
- ⅓ cup (65 grams) granulated sugar
- ⅓ cup packed (70 grams) light brown sugar
- 2 tablespoons whole milk
- ½ teaspoon pure vanilla extract
- ¼ teaspoon kosher salt
- ½ cup (90 grams) mini chocolate chips

ICE CREAM

- 6 large egg yolks
- 2 cups (455 grams) heavy cream
- 1 cup (225 grams) whole milk
- ½ cup (100 grams) granulated sugar
- 2 tablespoons light corn syrup
- Pinch of kosher salt
- 1 teaspoon pure vanilla extract

1 **Make the cookie dough:** Line a baking sheet with parchment paper.

2 Place the flour in a small microwave-safe bowl and microwave on high in 30-second intervals, stirring after each, for 2 minutes.

3 In a large bowl, combine the melted butter, granulated sugar, and brown sugar and beat with a handheld mixer on medium speed until light and fluffy, about 2 minutes. Add the flour, milk, vanilla, and salt and beat until combined, about 1 minute. Fold in the chocolate chips.

4 Drop teaspoonfuls of the dough onto the prepared baking sheet. Freeze until firm before using, about 1 hour, or transfer the dough bites to an airtight container and freeze for up to 3 months.

5 **Make the ice cream:** Place the egg yolks in a large heatproof bowl.

6 In a medium saucepan, whisk together the cream, milk, granulated sugar, corn syrup, and salt. Bring to a simmer over medium-high heat, then remove from the heat. While whisking continuously, slowly pour the hot cream mixture into the egg yolks and whisk until combined. Strain the mixture through a fine-mesh sieve into an airtight container and stir in the vanilla. Cover with the lid and refrigerate the custard until very cold, at least 4 hours or up to 24 hours.

7 Churn the chilled custard in an ice cream machine following the manufacturer's instructions. Transfer the ice cream to an airtight container and stir in the cookie dough bites, then cover with the lid and freeze until firm, about 4 hours. Store in the freezer for up to 3 months.

DONUTS

Apple Fritters

Makes 12

Apple fritters are the epitome of fall to me. To achieve the perfect texture—crispy on the outside, yet moist and tender on the inside—I use two spoons to loosely drop the batter into the oil. It gives them a rustic look with lots of craggy edges that get super crunchy. These fritters are also great with just a dusting of powdered sugar in lieu of the glaze.

FRITTERS

Neutral oil, such as avocado, sunflower, grapeseed, or canola oil, for frying

1½ cups (205 grams) gluten-free 1:1 replacement flour blend

¼ cup (50 grams) granulated sugar

1 teaspoon baking powder

¼ teaspoon kosher salt

1 cup (170 grams) buttermilk

1 large egg

2 tablespoons unsalted butter, melted

1 teaspoon pure vanilla extract

1 medium Granny Smith apple, peeled, cored, and diced (about 1 cup)

GLAZE

2 cups (225 grams) powdered sugar

2 tablespoons whole milk

1 teaspoon pure vanilla extract

1 **Make the fritters:** Fill a large pot with at least 1 inch of the oil and heat over medium heat to 350°F. Line a baking sheet with paper towels.

2 In a large bowl, whisk together the flour, granulated sugar, baking powder, and salt.

3 In a medium bowl, whisk together the buttermilk, egg, melted butter, and vanilla.

4 Make a well in the center of the dry ingredients. Add the wet ingredients to the well and stir until combined. Fold in the apples.

5 Working in batches, drop heaping ⅓-cup mounds of the dough into the hot oil and cook until golden, about 4 minutes, flipping them once halfway through. Using a slotted spoon, remove the fritters from the oil, shaking off any excess, and transfer to the paper towel–lined pan to cool. Repeat with the remaining dough, allowing the oil to return to 350°F between batches.

6 **Make the glaze:** In a large bowl or glass measuring cup, whisk together the powdered sugar, milk, and vanilla until smooth.

7 When the fritters are cool enough to handle, transfer them to a wire rack set over a rimmed baking sheet. Drizzle the glaze over the fritters and let dry completely before serving. Store, loosely covered, at room temperature for up to 3 days.

Chocolate Donut Holes

Makes
16 donut holes

In my family, Munchkins are the go-to treat to grab on the way to a playdate, party, or even soccer practice. These cake-style donut holes could not be easier to make at home and are ready in under an hour. But be warned: They're dangerous to have just lying around the house. I tend to pop one in my mouth every time I walk by, and by the end of the day, they're all gone!

DONUT HOLES

Neutral oil, such as avocado, sunflower, grapeseed, or canola oil

1⅓ cups (185 grams) gluten-free 1:1 replacement flour blend

⅓ cup (35 grams) unsweetened cocoa powder

¼ cup (50 grams) granulated sugar

1 teaspoon baking powder

¼ teaspoon kosher salt

¾ cup (170 grams) whole milk

1 large egg

1 teaspoon pure vanilla extract

GLAZE

2 cups (225 grams) powdered sugar

3 tablespoons whole milk

1 teaspoon pure vanilla extract

1 **Make the donut holes:** Fill a large pot with at least 1 inch of oil and heat over medium heat to 350°F. Line a baking sheet with paper towels.

2 In a large bowl, whisk together the flour, cocoa powder, granulated sugar, baking powder, and salt.

3 In a medium bowl, whisk together the milk, egg, 2 tablespoons of oil, and the vanilla. Make a well in the center of the dry ingredients, add the wet ingredients, and stir until combined.

4 Working in batches, drop 1½-tablespoons mounds of the dough into the hot oil and cook for 4 to 5 minutes, flipping them once halfway through. Using a slotted spoon, remove the donut holes from the oil, shaking off any excess, and transfer them to the paper towel–lined pan to cool. Repeat with the remaining dough, allowing the oil to return to 350°F between batches.

5 **Make the glaze:** In a large bowl, whisk together the powdered sugar, milk, and vanilla until smooth.

6 When the donut holes are cool enough to handle, dip each one in the glaze, rolling them to ensure the entire donut hole is coated. Transfer to a wire rack set over a rimmed baking sheet and let dry completely before serving. Store, loosely covered, at room temperature for up to 3 days.

Lemon Ricotta Donuts

Makes
10 donuts

I love lemon ricotta pancakes so I wanted to re-create that flavor profile into something for this book. The ricotta balances out the tartness of the lemon, and make these donuts rich, but not too dense. It's a unique custardy texture that you only get from adding ricotta to the otherwise pretty standard cake donut batter.

DONUTS

- Neutral oil, such as avocado, sunflower, grapeseed, or canola oil
- 1½ cups (205 grams) gluten-free 1:1 replacement flour blend
- 1 teaspoon baking powder
- ¼ teaspoon kosher salt
- 1 cup (220 grams) whole-milk ricotta
- 1 large egg
- ¼ cup (50 grams) granulated sugar
- Zest of 1 lemon (about 2 teaspoons)
- 1 teaspoon pure vanilla extract

GLAZE

- 2 cups (225 grams) powdered sugar
- 3 tablespoons fresh lemon juice
- 1 teaspoon pure vanilla extract
- Lemon zest, for garnish

1 **Make the donuts:** Fill a large pot with at least 1 inch of oil and heat over medium-high heat to 350°F. Line a baking sheet with paper towels.

2 In a medium bowl, whisk together the flour, baking powder, and salt.

3 In a large bowl, whisk together the ricotta, egg, granulated sugar, 2 tablespoons oil, the lemon zest, and the vanilla. Add the dry ingredients to the wet ingredients and stir until combined.

4 Working in batches, drop 3-tablespoon portions of the dough into the hot oil and cook until golden, 5 to 6 minutes, flipping them once halfway through. Using a slotted spoon, remove the donuts from the oil, shaking off any excess, and transfer to the paper towel–lined pan to cool. Repeat with the remaining dough, alowing the oil to return to 350°F between batches.

5 **Make the glaze:** In a large bowl, whisk together the powdered sugar, lemon juice, and vanilla until smooth.

6 When the donuts are cool enough to handle, dip each one in the glaze. Transfer to a wire rack set over a rimmed baking sheet, glazed-side up, and sprinkle with lemon zest. Let dry completely before serving. Store, loosely covered, at room temperature for up to 3 days.

Glazed Crullers

Makes
10 donuts

This is the next best thing to a Krispy Kreme. Warm from the fryer and freshly glazed, they have that perfectly crisp on the outside, creamy on the inside texture. My best trick for frying donuts, especially crullers, is to shape them on individual squares of parchment paper. That way you can use the paper to easily transfer them to the hot oil without accidentally deflating or misshaping the dough, or burning your hand.

CRULLERS

Neutral oil, such as avocado, sunflower, grapeseed, or canola oil, for frying

1 cup (140 grams) gluten-free 1:1 replacement flour blend

¼ cup (50 grams) granulated sugar

4 tablespoons (½ stick) unsalted butter

½ teaspoon kosher salt

1 large egg

GLAZE

2 cups (225 grams) powdered sugar

1 teaspoon pure vanilla extract

1 **Make the crullers:** Fill a large pot with at least 1 inch of the oil and heat over medium-high heat to 350°F. Line a baking sheet with paper towels. Cut ten 4-inch squares of parchment paper and place them on a second baking sheet.

2 Place the flour in the bowl of a stand mixer fitted with the whisk attachment.

3 In a large saucepan, combine the granulated sugar, butter, salt, and 1 cup (240 grams) water. Bring to a boil over medium-high heat. Pour the mixture over the flour and beat on medium-high speed until a smooth dough forms. Transfer the dough back to the saucepan and cook over medium heat, stirring, until the dough pulls away from the sides and forms a ball, about 5 minutes. Transfer the dough back to the bowl of the stand mixer. Beat on medium-high until slightly cooled, about 30 seconds, then beat in the egg. Transfer the dough to a piping bag fitted with a large star tip. Pipe a 2- to 3-inch circle of the dough onto each parchment square.

4 Carefully drop the dough circles into the hot oil, parchment-side up, and cook until golden, about 2 minutes, removing the parchment with tongs and flipping the crullers once halfway through. Using a slotted spoon, remove the crullers from the oil, shaking off any excess, and transfer to the paper towel–lined pan to cool. Repeat with the remaining dough, allowing the oil to return to 350°F between batches.

5 **Make the glaze:** In a large bowl, whisk together the powdered sugar, vanilla, and ¼ cup (60 grams) water until smooth.

6 When the crullers are cool enough to handle, dip each one in the glaze, flipping them once to ensure they are completely coated. Let the excess glaze drip off, then transfer the glazed cruller to a wire rack set over a rimmed baking sheet and let dry completely before serving. These are best served immediately, but you can store them, loosely covered, at room temperature for up to 3 days. Rewarm in the toaster oven before eating.

Nutella-Stuffed Beignets

Makes
16 beignets

When I studied pastry, beignets were one of the first things I learned to make, so they'll always have a special place in my heart. I stuffed these with Nutella because I love it as a dip for beignets, but this way, you don't have to serve it on the side—it all comes together in one neat little package. There's just something about the warm and gooey chocolate center that can't be beat.

- 1 cup (240 grams) warm water
- ¾ cup (170 grams) whole milk, warmed
- 1 (¼-ounce) packet active dry yeast (2¼ teaspoons)
- 2 tablespoons unsalted butter, melted
- 1 large egg
- 1 teaspoon pure vanilla extract
- 3¼ cups (450 grams) gluten-free 1:1 replacement flour blend, plus more for dusting
- 2 tablespoons ground psyllium husk (see page 11)
- ¼ cup (50 grams) granulated sugar
- 1½ teaspoons kosher salt
- Neutral oil, such as avocado, sunflower, grapeseed, or canola oil, for frying
- ½ cup (150 grams) chocolate-hazelnut spread, such as Nutella
- ¼ cup (30 grams) powdered sugar

1 In a medium bowl or large glass measuring cup, whisk together the warm water, milk, and yeast. Let stand for 5 minutes, until foamy. Add the melted butter, egg, and vanilla and whisk until combined.

2 In the bowl of a stand mixer fitted with the paddle attachment, combine the flour, psyllium husk, granulated sugar, and salt. With the mixer running on low speed, slowly pour in the wet mixture. Increase the speed to medium-low and beat until a smooth dough forms. Shape the dough into a ball at the bottom of the bowl, cover, and let stand until visibly risen and puffy, 1 to 1½ hours.

3 Line a baking sheet with parchment paper.

4 On a lightly floured surface, roll the dough out to a roughly 10-inch square, ½ inch thick. Using a pizza cutter, cut the dough into 16 squares. Transfer the beignets to the prepared pan, cover, and let rise until doubled in size, about 1 hour at room temperature or overnight in the fridge.

5 Fill a large pot with at least 3 inches of oil and heat over medium-high heat to 350°F. Line a baking sheet with paper towels.

6 Working in batches, transfer the beignets to the hot oil and cook until golden, about 6 minutes, flipping them once halfway through. Using a slotted spoon, remove the beignets from the oil, shaking off any excess, and transfer to the paper towel–lined pan to cool. Repeat with the remaining beignets, allowing the oil to return to 350°F between batches.

7 When the beignets are cool enough to handle, use a paring knife to pierce a horizontal hole in the side of each beignet.

8 Place the chocolate-hazelnut spread in a piping bag fitted with a Bismark tip or small round tip. Insert the tip into the hole in each beignet and fill with the chocolate-hazelnut spread. Dust with powdered sugar before serving. Store in an airtight container at room temperature for up to 3 days. Reheat in a toaster oven before serving.

Cinnamon-Sugar Yeast-Risen Baked Donuts

Makes 12 donuts

You don't need a donut pan to make donuts in your oven. This recipe uses a traditional yeast-leavened dough, but instead of frying the donuts, you bake them to save yourself the greasy mess. I love the simplicity of a cinnamon-sugar coating, but you can switch it up and top them with a glaze, if you prefer.

1¾ cups (400 grams) whole milk, warmed

1 (¼-ounce) packet active dry yeast (2¼ teaspoons)

2 tablespoons unsalted butter, melted

1 large egg

1 teaspoon pure vanilla extract

3¼ cups (450 grams) gluten-free 1:1 replacement flour blend, plus more for dusting

2 tablespoons ground psyllium husk (see page 11)

¾ cup (150 grams) sugar

1½ teaspoons kosher salt

1 tablespoon ground cinnamon

Nonstick cooking spray

1 In a medium bowl or large glass measuring cup, whisk together the milk and yeast. Let stand for 5 minutes, until foamy. Add the melted butter, egg, and vanilla and whisk until combined.

2 In the bowl of a stand mixer fitted with the paddle attachment, combine the flour, psyllium husk, ¼ cup (50 grams) of the sugar, and the salt. With the mixer running on low speed, slowly pour in the milk mixture. Increase the speed to medium-low and beat until a smooth dough forms, about 1 minute. Shape the dough into a ball at the bottom of the bowl, cover, and let stand until visibly risen and puffy, 1 to 1½ hours.

3 Line two baking sheets with parchment paper.

4 On a lightly floured surface, roll the dough out to ½-inch thickness. Cut donuts using a donut cutter, or use a 3- to 4-inch round cookie cutter and cut out the centers using the wide end of a large piping tip. Smush the dough scraps together, reroll, and cut out more donuts until you've used as much dough as possible. You should have about 12 donuts. Transfer the donuts to the prepared baking sheets and cover. Let rise until doubled in size, about 1 hour at room temperature or overnight in the fridge.

5 Preheat the oven 350°F. In a shallow bowl, combine the remaining ½ cup (100 grams) sugar and the cinnamon.

6 Bake the donuts for about 30 minutes, until golden. Let cool until cool enough to handle, 5 to 10 minutes, then spray each donut with cooking spray and dip them in the cinnamon-sugar mixture, turning them to coat completely. These are best served the day they are made, but you can store them, loosely covered, at room temperature for up to 2 days. Rewarm them slightly in the microwave or a toaster oven before serving.

Baked Chocolate-Glazed Donuts

Makes
12 donuts

If Leni and Ella could choose breakfast every morning, this would be it: a simple vanilla cake donut topped with a chocolaty glaze. I love that these donuts are so simple to make that if the kids want them, they can help me whip up a batch. It's a fun family weekend baking project that doesn't have me pulling my hair out.

DONUTS

Nonstick cooking spray

1½ cups (205 grams) gluten-free 1:1 replacement flour blend

1 teaspoon baking powder

¼ teaspoon kosher salt

1 cup (225 grams) whole milk

1 large egg

¼ cup (50 grams) granulated sugar

2 tablespoons neutral oil, such as avocado, sunflower, grapeseed, or canola oil

1 teaspoon pure vanilla extract

ICING

1½ cups (170 grams) powdered sugar

3 tablespoons whole milk

1 tablespoon unsweetened cocoa powder

½ teaspoon pure vanilla extract

1 **Make the donuts:** Preheat the oven to 350°F. Coat two 6-donut donut pans with cooking spray.

2 In a medium bowl, whisk together the flour, baking powder, and salt.

3 In a large bowl, whisk together the milk, egg, granulated sugar, oil, and vanilla. Add the dry ingredients to the wet ingredients and stir until combined.

4 Transfer the batter to a large zip-top bag and snip one corner off, creating a ½-inch hole. Pipe the batter into the prepared donut pans. Bake for 15 minutes, until the donuts are golden and a toothpick inserted into the center comes out with just a few moist crumbs attached. Let cool completely, about 1 hour.

5 **Make the icing:** In a large bowl, whisk together the powdered sugar, milk, cocoa powder, and vanilla until smooth.

6 Dip the top of each donut into the icing, then transfer to a wire rack set over a rimmed baking sheet. Let set until the icing is dry to the touch, about 30 minutes. Store in an airtight container at room temperature for up to 3 days.

Stuffed Churros

Makes
16 churros

This one-ingredient dulce de leche takes a long time to cook, but it is oh so worth it. The sweetened condensed milk gets more and more caramelized the longer you cook it—just make sure you keep the can fully submerged in water the whole time it cooks so it doesn't explode. Store leftovers in the fridge to use for dipping apple slices, spreading on graham crackers, or drizzling atop oatmeal.

- 1 (14-ounce) can sweetened condensed milk
- 1¼ cups (175 grams) gluten-free 1:1 replacement flour blend
- 1¼ cups (250 grams) sugar
- 4 tablespoons (½ stick) unsalted butter
- ½ teaspoon kosher salt
- 1 large egg
- Neutral oil, such as avocado, sunflower, grapeseed, or canola oil, for frying
- 1 tablespoon ground cinnamon

1 Place the unopened can of condensed milk in a large pot and add water to cover by at least 2 inches. Bring the water to a boil over medium-high heat and cook, adding water as needed to keep the can completely covered at all times, for 2 hours. Using tongs, carefully remove the can from the water and set aside to cool completely, about 4 hours.

2 Line a baking sheet with parchment paper. Place the flour in the bowl of a stand mixer fitted with the whisk attachment.

3 In a large saucepan, combine 1 cup (240 grams) water, ¾ cup (150 grams) of the sugar, the butter, and the salt. Bring to a boil over medium-high heat. Pour the mixture over the flour and beat on medium-high speed until a smooth dough forms, about 1 minute.

4 Transfer the dough back to the saucepan and cook over medium heat, stirring, until the dough pulls away from the sides of the pan and forms a ball, about 5 minutes. Transfer the dough back to the stand mixer bowl and beat on medium-high until slightly cooled, about 30 seconds, then beat in the egg. Transfer the dough to a piping bag fitted with a large star tip. Pipe 5-inch-long lines of batter onto the prepared baking sheet and freeze until firm, at least 1 hour.

5 Fill a large pot with at least 1 inch of oil and heat over medium heat to 350°F. Line a baking sheet with paper towels. In a shallow bowl, combine the remaining ½ cup (100 grams) sugar and the cinnamon.

6 Working in batches, carefully drop the frozen dough into the hot oil and cook until puffed into cylinders and golden, 3 to 4 minutes. Using a slotted spoon, remove the churros from the oil,

Recipe continues

shaking off any excess, and transfer them to the paper towel–lined pan to cool. Repeat with the remaining dough, allowing the oil to return to 350°F between batches.

7 When the churros are cool enough to handle, transfer them to the bowl with the cinnamon-sugar mixture and toss to coat completely, then return the coated churros to the baking sheet. Using a skewer, pierce a hole lengthwise through the center of each churro.

8 Open the can of condensed milk and transfer half the dulce de leche to a piping bag fitted with a Bismark tip or small round tip (transfer the remaining dulce de leche to an airtight container and store in the refrigerator for up to 1 week for another use). Insert the tip of the piping bag into the hole in each churro and fill with the dulce de leche.

9 These are best served immediately but can be stored in an airtight container in the refrigerator for up to 3 days. Rewarm in a toaster oven before eating.

DOH!nuts

Makes
12 donuts

Every time I watch *The Simpsons* I can't help but crave a donut—specifically a vanilla donut topped with pink glaze and rainbow sprinkles—so I decided to make a recipe I can whip up any time I'm jumping into one of my favorite episodes. A wide-mouthed mason jar lid ring is the perfect tool for cutting out the donuts. It's about ½ inch thick (the ideal thickness for the rolled-out dough) and 3½ inches in diameter, the perfect donut size.

DONUTS

- 1¾ cups (400 grams) whole milk, warmed
- 1 (¼-ounce) packet active dry yeast (2¼ teaspoons)
- 2 tablespoons unsalted butter, melted
- 1 large egg
- 1 teaspoon pure vanilla extract
- 3¼ cups (450 grams) gluten-free 1:1 replacement flour blend, plus more for dusting
- 2 tablespoons ground psyllium husk (see page 11)
- ¼ cup (50 grams) granulated sugar
- 1½ teaspoons kosher salt
- Neutral oil, such as avocado, sunflower, grapeseed, or canola oil, for frying

GLAZE

- 4 cups (455 grams) powdered sugar
- 6 tablespoons (85 grams) whole milk
- 2 teaspoons pure vanilla extract
- 2 drops pink gel food coloring
- Rainbow sprinkles

1 **Make the donuts:** In a medium bowl or large glass measuring cup, whisk together the milk and yeast. Let stand for 5 minutes, until foamy. Add the melted butter, egg, and vanilla and whisk until combined.

2 In the bowl of a stand mixer fitted with the paddle attachment, combine the flour, psyllium husk, granulated sugar, and salt. With the mixer running on low speed, slowly pour in the wet mixture. Increase the speed to medium-low and beat until a smooth dough forms, about 3 minutes. Shape the dough into a ball at the bottom of the bowl, cover, and let stand until visibly risen and puffy, 1 to 1½ hours.

3 Cut twelve 4-inch square pieces of parchment paper and place them in a single layer on two baking sheets.

4 On a lightly floured surface, roll out the dough to ½-inch thickness. Cut out donuts using a donut cutter, a 3- to 4-inch round cookie cutter, or a mason jar lid ring and cut out the centers using the wide end of a large piping tip. Smush the dough scraps together, reroll, and cut out more donuts until you've used as much dough as possible. You should have about 12 donuts. Transfer each donut to a parchment square, cover with a tea towel, and let rise until doubled in size, about 1 hour at room temperature or overnight in the fridge.

5 Fill a large pot with at least 1 inch of the oil and heat over medium-high heat to 350°F. Line a baking sheet with paper towels.

Recipe continues

6 Working in batches, transfer the donuts to the hot oil and cook until golden, about 4 minutes, flipping them once halfway through. Using a slotted spoon, remove the donuts from the oil, shaking off any excess, and transfer to the paper towel–lined pan to cool. Repeat with the remaining donuts, allowing the oil to return to 350°F between batches.

7 **Make the glaze:** In a large bowl, whisk together the powdered sugar, milk, vanilla, and food coloring until smooth.

8 When the donuts are cooled enough to handle, dip each one in the glaze and transfer to a wire rack to set. When the glaze has set, dip each donut a second time, then immediately garnish with the sprinkles. Return the donuts to the rack to set until dried. These are best served on the day they are made, but you can store them, loosely covered, at room temperature for up to 2 days. Rewarm them slightly in the microwave before serving.

Acknowledgments

Devon: My gluten-free goddess. What a journey it has been!! Getting to know you throughout the process of making this cookbook has been one of the best takeaways of this entire experience. Your knowledge and passion for the craft of gluten-free baking have helped shape this book into the best cookbook and resource it can be. I'm so grateful for your hard work, attention to detail, and dedication to making sure every recipe was perfect through and through. Forever grateful—this book wouldn't be the same without you.

Morgan: Your creativity, eye for detail, and ability to bring my vision to life was more than I could have ever imagined. The photos in this book surpass my wildest expectations. I'm so grateful for you and the team you put together, your expertise, and your dedication throughout this entire process.

Judy, Ashleigh, Debbie, Takako, and Maeve: What we accomplished in less than two weeks is unreal! From every recipe to every setup and everything in between, your creativity is unmatched, and your talent knows no bounds!!! I feel so lucky to have been able to share this experience with all of you.

Caitlin, Renée, and the entire Union Square & Co. team: Thank you for your hard work, dedication, and expertise throughout this journey. From the first draft to the final print, your support and guidance have been invaluable. I'm so grateful for your attention to detail, your belief in this project, and your commitment to making it as amazing as it is.

Brandi: This being our second book together, I'm reminded once again of how lucky I am to have you in my corner. Your guidance, expertise, and commitment have been instrumental in getting this book into the world and into the right hands.

Adam: My partner and my rock. Thank you for your endless support and for holding down the fort so I can continue to pursue my dreams and create something as special as this cookbook. Thank you for always being there, tasting my recipes, offering your honest feedback, and

believing in me since day one. Most important, THANK YOU for being so cool when we had a team of people take over our house for two weeks while we shot this cookbook!!

Leni and Ella: You two are my greatest inspirations. Your laughter, curiosity, and love are a constant reminder of why I love to bake and the importance of making memories in the kitchen. You've been my little taste-testers, my helpers, and my biggest supporters throughout this entire journey. I love you more than you will ever know, and I am so proud to be your mom.

Ceres: Thank you for always keeping it clean and offering to help whenever I needed it! You have been an asset from day one. The entire team and I are so appreciative!

Mom, Dad, Jamie, Age, and Scott: I couldn't do any of this without your constant support. From our daily phone calls to photo shoot visits, getting to run things by all of you on a whim, and getting to share the play-by-play with you in real time as things progressed was one of the best parts of this entire experience. I love you guys forever and always.

Index

Note: Page references in *italic* indicate photographs.

A

Almond Croissants, 100
Apple & Brie Galette, 174, *175*
Apple Cinnamon Baked Oats, 106, *107*
Apple Fritters, *212*, 213
Apple Pie, Grandma Doris's, 178–180, *179*
apples
- Apple & Brie Galette, 174, *175*
- Apple Cinnamon Baked Oats, 106, *107*
- Apple Fritters, *212*, 213
- Frangipane Fruit Tart, *164*, 165
- Grandma Doris's Apple Pie, 178–180, *179*

B

babka
- Babka French Toast, 86, 87
- Chocolate Babka, 80, 81–82

Babka French Toast, *86*, 87
bagels
- Savory Bagels, *74*, *94*, 95
- Speedy Bagels, *74*, *94*, 95
- Sweet Bagels, *74*, *94*, 95

Baked Chocolate-Glazed Donuts, *210*, *224*, 225
bananas
- Banana Split Pudding Pops, *190*, 191
- Upside-Down Bananas Foster Cake, *64*, 65

Bananas Foster Cake, Upside-Down, *64*, 65
Banana Split Pudding Pops, *190*, 191
bars, 109–129
- Brown Butter Rice Crispy Treats, 116, *117*
- Cheesecake Swirl Brownies, *122*, 123
- Chocolate Chunk Brown Butter Blondies, 124, *125*
- Chocolate Mint Brownies, 128, *129*
- Cookies & Cream Rice Crispy Treats, 116, *117*
- Frosted Sugar Cookie Bars, *108*, 120, *121*
- Fruity Rice Crispy Treats, 116, *117*
- Oreo Cheesecake Bars, *118*, 119
- Peach Crumble Bars, *126*, 127
- Rainbow Chocolate Chip Granola Bars, *110*, 111
- Scotcheroos, *114*, 115
- S'mores Brownies, 112, *113*

batter
- Brownie Batter Ice Cream, *206*, 207
- Cake Batter Macarons, 36–37, *37*

Beignets, Nutella-Stuffed, *220*, 221
Birthday Cake, Confetti, *8*, 52, *53*
Black & White Cookies, 24, *25*
Blondies, Chocolate Chunk Brown Butter, 124, *125*
Blueberry Crumble, Skillet, *176*, 177
Boston Cream Cupcakes, *130*, *152*, 153–154
Bread, Sourdough, 101–102, *103*
breads, 75–107
- Apple Cinnamon Baked Oats, 106, *107*
- Babka French Toast, *86*, 87
- Challah Bread Pudding, 88, *89*
- Challah, 96, *97*
- Chocolate Babka, *80*, 81–82
- Chocolate Swirl Pumpkin Bread, *76*, 77
- Cinnamon Morning Buns, 83–84, *85*
- Cranberry-Orange Scones, *104*, 105
- Croissants, *98*, 99–100
- Pull-Apart Cinnamon Bread, *92*, *93*
- Soft Pretzels, 78, *79*
- Sourdough Bread, 101–102, *103*
- Speedy Bagels, *74*, *94*, 95
- Zucchini Bread, *90*, 91

Brie Galette, Apple &, 174, *175*
brown butter
- Brown Butter Rice Crispy Treats, 116, 117
- Chocolate Chunk Brown Butter Blondies, 124, 125

Brown Butter Rice Crispy Treats, 116, *117*
Brownie Batter Ice Cream, *206*, 207
brownies
- Brownie Batter Ice Cream, *206*, 207
- Cheesecake Swirl Brownies, *122*, 123
- Chocolate Mint Brownies, 128, *129*
- S'mores Brownies, 112, *113*

Bundt Cake, Neapolitan, *2*, 70–71, *71*
Bundt cakes
- Neapolitan Bundt Cake, *2*, 70–71, *71*
- Pull-Apart Cinnamon Bread, *92*, *93*

buttermilk
Apple Fritters, *212*, 213
Black & White Cookies, 24, *25*
Chocolate Swirl Pumpkin Bread, *76*, 77
Cranberry-Orange Scones, *104*, 105
Red Velvet Cake, *50*, 51
Red Velvet Ice Cream Sandwiches, 202, 204, 205
Red Velvet Ice Cream, 192, *193*
substitutions, 15
Zucchini Bread, *90*, 91
butter substitutions, 15

C

Cake Batter Macarons, 36–37, *37*
Cake, Carrot, 61–62, *63*
Cake, Chocolate Layer, *48*, *72*, 73
Cake, Confetti Birthday, *8*, 52, *53*
Cake Cupcakes, White, *144*, 145
Cake, Dirt Cup Poke, 66, *67*
Cake, Flourless Peanut Butter–Chocolate Mug, 56, *57*
Cake, Neapolitan Bundt, *2*, 70–71, *71*
Cake, Red Velvet, *50*, 51
cakes, 49–73
Carrot Cake, 61–62, *63*
Chocolate Layer Cake, *48*, *72*, 73
Confetti Birthday Cake, *8*, 52, *53*
Dirt Cup Poke Cake, 66, *67*
Flourless Peanut Butter–Chocolate Mug Cake, 56, *57*
Neapolitan Bundt Cake, *2*, 70–71, *71*
Raspberry Swirl Cheesecake, *68*, 69
Red Velvet Cake, *50*, 51
Strawberries & Cream Cake, *54*, 55
Tiramisu Trifle, *58*, 59–60
Upside-Down Bananas Foster Cake, *64*, 65
Cake, Strawberries & Cream, *54*, 55
Cake, Upside-Down Bananas Foster, *64*, 65
Cannoli Cones, *148*, 149
Caputo, 11
caramel
Caramel Chocolate Pie, Coconut, *168*, 169
Millionaire's Cupcakes, 155–156, *157*
Stuffed Churros, 226–228, *227*
Caramel Chocolate Pie, Coconut, *168*, 169
Carrot Cake, 61–62, *63*
cereal, 11
Brown Butter Rice Crispy Treats, 116, *117*
Cookies & Cream Rice Crispy Treats, 116, *117*
Fruity Rice Crispy Treats, 116, *117*
Lucky Charms Cereal Cookies, 28, *29*
Scotcheroos, *114*, 115
challah
Challah, 96, *97*
Challah Bread Pudding, 88, *89*
cheesecake
Cheesecake Swirl Brownies, *122*, 123
Oreo Cheesecake Bars, 118, 119
Raspberry Swirl Cheesecake, 68, 69
Strawberry Cheesecake Cupcakes, 132, 133
Cheesecake Bars, Oreo, *118*, 119
Cheesecake Cupcakes, Strawberry, *132*, 133
Cheesecake, Raspberry Swirl, *68*, 69
Cheesecake Swirl Brownies, *122*, 123
Cherry Pie, Sour, *4–5*, 162, *163*
chocolate
Babka French Toast, *86*, 87
Baked Chocolate-Glazed Donuts, *210*, *224*, 225
Banana Split Pudding Pops, *190*, 191
Black & White Cookies, 24, *25*
Boston Cream Cupcakes, *130*, *152*, 153–154
Brownie Batter Ice Cream, *206*, 207
Cheesecake Swirl Brownies, *122*, 123
Chocolate Babka, *80*, 81–82
Chocolate Chunk Brown Butter Blondies, 124, *125*
Chocolate Donut Holes, 214, *215*
Chocolate Espresso Cookies, *34*, 35
Chocolate Fluffernutter Pie, *158*, 166, *167*
Chocolate Layer Cake, *48*, *72*, 73
Chocolate Mint Brownies, 128, *129*
Chocolate Pecan Pie, 181–183, *182*
Chocolate Shortbread Cookies, *42*, 43
Chocolate Swirl Pumpkin Bread, *76*, 77
Chocolate Zucchini Cupcakes, 146, *147*
Chocolate-Covered Strawberry Macarons, *46*, 47
Coconut Caramel Chocolate Pie, *168*, 169
Cookies & Cream Cupcakes, 134, *135*
Cookies & Cream Ice Cream Sandwiches, 204, *205*
Cookies & Cream Ice Cream, 188, *189*

chocolate (*continued*)
- Cosmic No-Bake Cookies, *22*, 23
- Cream-Filled Chocolate Cupcakes, *138*, 139–140
- Crispy Chocolate Chip Cookies, 40, *41*
- Dark Chocolate Sandwich Cookies, *26*, 27
- Dirt Cup Poke Cake, 66, *67*
- Flourless Peanut Butter–Chocolate Mug Cake, 56, *57*
- Ice Cream Sandwiches, *202*, 203–204, *205*
- Mandel Bread, 32, *33*
- Millionaire's Cupcakes, 155–156, *157*
- Neapolitan Bundt Cake, *2*, 70–71, *71*
- Nutella Fudge Pops, *186*, 187
- Nutella-Stuffed Beignets, *220*, 221
- Oreo Cheesecake Bars, *118*, 119
- Rainbow Chocolate Chip Granola Bars, *110*, 111
- Rocky Road Cookies, *30*, 31
- Scotcheroos, *114*, 115
- S'mores Brownies, 112, *113*

Chocolate Babka, *80*, 81–82
Chocolate Chip Cookies, Crispy, 40, *41*
Chocolate Chip Granola Bars, Rainbow, *110*, 111
Chocolate Chip Granola, Rainbow, 111
Chocolate Chunk Brown Butter Blondies, 124, *125*
Chocolate Cupcakes, Cream-Filled, *138*, 139–140
Chocolate Donut Holes, 214, *215*
Chocolate Espresso Cookies, *34*, 35
Chocolate Fluffernutter Pie, *158*, 166, *167*
Chocolate Layer Cake, *48*, *72*, 73
Chocolate Mint Brownies, 128, *129*
Chocolate Pecan Pie, 181–183, *182*
Chocolate Shortbread Cookies, *42*, 43
Chocolate Swirl Pumpkin Bread, *76*, 77
Chocolate Zucchini Cupcakes, 146, *147*
Chocolate-Glazed Donuts, Baked, *210*, *224*, 225
Chocolate-Covered Strawberry Macarons, *46*, 47
Churros, Stuffed, 226–228, *227*
cinnamon
- Apple Cinnamon Baked Oats, 106, *107*
- Cinnamon Morning Buns, 83–84, *85*
- Cinnamon-Sugar Yeast-Risen Baked Donuts, 222, *223*
- Pull-Apart Cinnamon Bread, 92, *93*
- Sweet Potato Cinnamon Cupcakes, 150, *151*

Cinnamon Bread, Pull-Apart, 92, *93*
Cinnamon Morning Buns, 83–84, *85*
Cinnamon-Sugar Yeast-Risen Baked Donuts, 222, *223*
coconut
- Coconut Caramel Chocolate Pie, *168*, 169
- Rainbow Chocolate Chip Granola Bars, *110*, 111

Coconut Caramel Chocolate Pie, *168*, 169
coffee
- Chocolate Espresso Cookies, *34*, 35
- No-Churn Coffee Ice Cream, 200, *201*

Coffee Ice Cream, No-Churn, 200, *201*
Confetti Birthday Cake, *8*, 52, *53*
Confetti Shortbread Cookies, *42*, 43
Cookie Dough Ice Cream, 208, *209*
cookies, 17–47
- Black & White Cookies, 24, *25*
- Cake Batter Macarons, 36–37, *37*
- Chocolate Espresso Cookies, *34*, 35
- Chocolate Shortbread Cookies, *42*, 43
- Chocolate-Covered Strawberry Macarons, *46*, 47
- Confetti Shortbread Cookies, *42*, 43
- Cosmic No-Bake Cookies, *22*, 23
- Crispy Chocolate Chip Cookies, 40, *41*
- Cut-Out Sugar Cookies, 44, *45*
- Dark Chocolate Sandwich Cookies, *26*, 27
- Lucky Charms Cereal Cookies, *28*, *29*
- Mandel Bread, 32, *33*
- Oatmeal Raisin Cookies, *38*, 39
- Rocky Road Cookies, *30*, 31
- Strawberry Shortcake Cookies, *18*, 19
- Stuffed Fluffernutter Cookies, 20, *21*

cookies and cream
- Cookies & Cream Cupcakes, 134, *135*
- Cookies & Cream Ice Cream, 188, *189*
- Cookies & Cream Ice Cream Sandwiches, 204, *205*
- Cookies & Cream Rice Crispy Treats, 116, *117*

Cookies & Cream Cupcakes, 134, *135*
Cookies & Cream Ice Cream, 188, *189*
Cookies & Cream Ice Cream Sandwiches, 204, *205*
Cookies & Cream Rice Crispy Treats, 116, *117*
Cosmic No-Bake Cookies, *22*, 23
Cranberry-Orange Scones, *104*, 105

Cream-Filled Chocolate Cupcakes, *138*, 139–140
Crème Brûlée Cupcakes, 141–142, *143*
Crispy Chocolate Chip Cookies, 40, *41*
Croissants, *98*, 99–100
Croissants, Almond, 100
Crookies, 100
Crullers, Glazed, 218, *219*
Crumble Bars, Peach, *126*, 127
cupcakes, 131–157
  Boston Cream Cupcakes, *130*, *152*, 153–154
  Cannoli Cones, *148*, 149
  Chocolate Zucchini Cupcakes, 146, *147*
  Cookies & Cream Cupcakes, 134, *135*
  Cream-Filled Chocolate Cupcakes, *138*, 139–140
  Crème Brûlée Cupcakes, 141–142, *143*
  Lemon Cupcakes, *136*, 137
  Millionaire's Cupcakes, 155–156, *157*
  Strawberry Cheesecake Cupcakes, *132*, 133
  Sweet Potato Cinnamon Cupcakes, 150, *151*
  White Cake Cupcakes, *144*, 145
Cup4Cup, 11
Cut-Out Sugar Cookies, 44, *45*

D

dairy substitutions, 15
Dark Chocolate Sandwich Cookies, *26*, 27
Dirt Cup Poke Cake, 66, *67*
DOH!nuts, 229–230, *231*
donuts, 211–231
  Apple Fritters, *212*, 213
  Baked Chocolate-Glazed Donuts, *210*, *224*, 225
  Chocolate Donut Holes, 214, *215*
  Cinnamon-Sugar Yeast-Risen Baked Donuts, 222, *223*
  DOH!nuts, 229–230, *231*
  Glazed Crullers, 218, *219*
  Lemon Ricotta Donuts, *216*, 217
  Nutella-Stuffed Beignets, *220*, 221
  Stuffed Churros, 226–228, *227*
donut holes
  Chocolate Donut Holes, 214, *215*
  Lemon Ricotta Donuts, *216*, 217
Donuts, Baked, 222, *223*
Donuts, Baked Chocolate-Glazed, 210, 224, 225
Donuts, Lemon Ricotta, 216, 217
dulce de leche, 226–228

E

egg substitutions, 15
egg wash, 15
egg white substitutions, 15
Espresso Cookies, Chocolate, *34*, 35

F

flour blends, 11
Flourless Peanut Butter–Chocolate Mug Cake, 56, *57*
Fluff
  Chocolate Fluffernutter Pie, *158*, 166, 167
  Cream-Filled Chocolate Cupcakes, *138*, 139–140
  S'mores Brownies, 112, *113*
  Stuffed Fluffernutter Cookies, 20, *21*
Fluffernutter Pie, Chocolate, *158*, 166, *167*
Fluffernutter Cookies, Stuffed, 20, *21*
Frangipane Fruit Tart, *164*, 165
French Toast, Babka, *86*, 87
Fritters, Apple, *212*, 213
Frosted Sugar Cookie Bars, *108*, 120, *121*
fruits
  Apple & Brie Galette, 174, *175*
  Apple Cinnamon Baked Oats, 106, *107*
  Apple Fritters, *212*, 213
  Banana Split Pudding Pops, *190*, 191
  Chocolate-Covered Strawberry Macarons, *46*, 47
  Cranberry-Orange Scones, *104*, 105
  Frangipane Fruit Tart, *164*, 165
  Grandma Doris's Apple Pie, 178–180, *179*
  Grapefruit Sorbet, 199
  Lemon Cupcakes, *136*, 137
  Lemon Poppy Seed Tart, *14*, *172*, 173
  Lemon Ricotta Donuts, *216*, 217
  Lemon Sorbet, *184*, 199
  Orange Sorbet, *198*, 199
  Peach Crumble Bars, *126*, 127
  Pineapple Whip, *194*, 195
  Raspberry Swirl Cheesecake, *68*, 69
  Red Wine Pear Tart, 170, *171*
  Skillet Blueberry Crumble, *176*, 177
  Sour Cherry Pie, *4–5*, 162, *163*
  Stone Fruit Galette, *160*, 161
  Strawberries & Cream Cake, *54*, 55
  Strawberry Cheesecake Cupcakes, *132*, 133
  Strawberry Shortcake Cookies, *18*, 19
  Upside-Down Bananas Foster Cake, *64*, 65
Fruit Tart, Frangipane, *164*, 165
Fruity Rice Crispy Treats, 116, *117*
Fudge Pops, Nutella, *186*, 187

G

Galette, Apple & Brie, 174, *175*
Galette, Stone Fruit, *160*, 161
galettes
  Apple & Brie Galette, 174, *175*
  Stone Fruit Galette, *160*, 161
Glazed Crullers, 218, *219*
gluten-free cereals, 11
gluten-free flour blends, 11
gluten-free ingredients, 11
gluten-free 1:1 replacement flour blend, 11
gluten-free wheat starch, 11
Grandma Doris's Apple Pie, 178–180, *179*
granola
  Rainbow Chocolate Chip Granola, 111
  Rainbow Chocolate Chip Granola Bars, *110*, 111
Grapefruit Sorbet, 199
grittiness, 12

H

honey substitutions, 15
hydration time, 12

I

ice cream, 185–209
  Banana Split Pudding Pops, *190*, 191
  Brownie Batter Ice Cream, *206*, 207
  Cookie Dough Ice Cream, 208, *209*
  Cookies & Cream Ice Cream Sandwiches, 204, *205*
  Cookies & Cream Ice Cream, 188, *189*
  Grapefruit Sorbet, 199
  Ice Cream Sandwiches, *202*, 203–204, *205*
  Lemon Sorbet, *184*, 199
  Mango Whip, *194*, 195
  No-Churn Coffee Ice Cream, 200, *201*
  Nutella Fudge Pops, *186*, 187
  Orange Sorbet, *198*, 199
  Pineapple Whip, *194*, 195
  Rainbow Sherbet, 196, *197*
  Red Velvet Ice Cream Sandwiches, *202*, 204, *205*
  Red Velvet Ice Cream, 192, *193*
  Strawberry Whip, *194*, 195
ice cream sandwiches
  Cookies & Cream Ice Cream Sandwiches, 204, *205*
  Ice Cream Sandwiches, *202*, 203–204, *205*
  Red Velvet Ice Cream Sandwiches, 202, 204, 205

K

key ingredients, 11
King Arthur, 11
kitchen scale, 12
kneading, 12

L

layer cakes
  Chocolate Layer Cake, *48*, *72*, 73
  Confetti Birthday Cake, *8*, 52, *53*
  Red Velvet Cake, *50*, 51
  Strawberries & Cream Cake, *54*, 55
lemon
  Lemon Cupcakes, *136*, 137
  lemon curd, 137, 173
  Lemon Poppy Seed Tart, *14*, *172*, 173
  Lemon Ricotta Donuts, *216*, 217
  Lemon Sorbet, *184*, 199
Lemon Cupcakes, *136*, 137
lemon curd, 137, 173
Lemon Poppy Seed Tart, *14*, *172*, 173
Lemon Ricotta Donuts, *216*, 217
Lemon Sorbet, *184*, 199
lining pans, 13
Lucky Charms Cereal Cookies, *28*, *29*

M

macarons
  Cake Batter Macarons, 36–37, *37*
  Chocolate-Covered Strawberry Macarons, *46*, 47
Malt-O-Meal, 11
Mandel Bread, 32, *33*
Mango Whip, *194*, 195
Milano cookies, 27
milk substitutions, 15
Millionaire's Cupcakes, 155–156, *157*
Mint Brownies, Chocolate, 128, *129*
Morning Buns, Cinnamon, 83–84, *85*
muffin cup liners, 13
Mug Cake, Flourless Peanut Butter–Chocolate, 56, 57

N

Neapolitan Bundt Cake, *2*, 70–71, *71*
No-Bake Cookies, Cosmic, *22*, 23
No-Churn Coffee Ice Cream, 200, *201*
Nutella
  Nutella Fudge Pops, *186*, 187
  Nutella-Stuffed Beignets, *220*, 221
Nutella Fudge Pops, *186*, 187
Nutella-Stuffed Beignets, *220*, 221

O

Oatmeal Raisin Cookies, *38*, 39
oats, 11
  Apple Cinnamon Baked Oats, 106, *107*

Oatmeal Raisin Cookies, *38*, 39
1:1 replacement flour blend, 11
orange
Cranberry-Orange Scones, *104*, 105
Orange Sorbet, *198*, 199
Orange Scones, Cranberry-, *104*, 105
Orange Sorbet, *198*, 199
Oreo Cheesecake Bars, *118*, 119
Oreos
Chocolate Fluffernutter Pie, *158*, 166, *167*
Cookies & Cream Cupcakes, 134, *135*
Cookies & Cream Ice Cream, 188, *189*
Cookies & Cream Ice Cream Sandwiches, 204, *205*
Cookies & Cream Rice Crispy Treats, 116, *117*
Dirt Cup Poke Cake, 66, *67*
Oreo Cheesecake Bars, *118*, 119
overmixing, 13

P

pans, lining, 13
parchment paper, 13
Peach Crumble Bars, *126*, 127
peaches
Peach Crumble Bars, *126*, 127
Stone Fruit Galette, *160*, 161
Skillet Blueberry Crumble, *176*, 177
Peanut Butter–Chocolate Mug Cake, Flourless, 56, *57*
Pear Tart, Red Wine, 170, *171*
Pecan Pie, Chocolate, 181–183, *182*
pies, 159–183
Apple & Brie Galette, 174, *175*
Chocolate Fluffernutter Pie, *158*, 166, *167*
Chocolate Pecan Pie, 181–183, *182*
Coconut Caramel Chocolate Pie, *168*, 169
Frangipane Fruit Tart, *164*, 165
Grandma Doris's Apple Pie, 178–180, *179*
Lemon Poppy Seed Tart, *14*, *172*, 173
Red Wine Pear Tart, 170, *171*
Skillet Blueberry Crumble, *176*, 177
Sour Cherry Pie, *4–5*, 162, *163*
Stone Fruit Galette, *160*, 161
Pineapple Whip, *194*, 195
Poke Cake, Dirt Cup, 66, *67*
Poppy Seed Tart, Lemon, *14*, *172*, 173
Pretzels, Soft, 78, *79*
psyllium husk, 11
Pudding Pops, Banana Split, *190*, 191
Pull-Apart Cinnamon Bread, 92, *93*
Pumpkin Bread, Chocolate Swirl, *76*, 77

R

Rainbow Chocolate Chip Granola Bars, *110*, 111
Rainbow Sherbet, 196, *197*
raisins
Oatmeal Raisin Cookies, *38*, 39
Sweet Bagels, *74*, *94*, 95
Raspberry Swirl Cheesecake, *68*, 69
red velvet
Red Velvet Cake, *50*, 51
Red Velvet Ice Cream, 192, *193*
Red Velvet Ice Cream Sandwiches, 202, 204, 205
Red Velvet Cake, *50*, 51
Red Velvet Ice Cream, 192, *193*
Red Velvet Ice Cream Sandwiches, 202, 204, 205
Red Wine Pear Tart, 170, *171*
replacement flour blend, 1:1, 11
rice crispy treats
Brown Butter Rice Crispy Treats, 116, *117*
Cookies & Cream Rice Crispy Treats, 116, *117*
Fruity Rice Crispy Treats, 116, *117*
Rice Crispy Treats, Brown Butter, 116, *117*
ricotta
Cannoli Cones, *148*, 149
Lemon Ricotta Donuts, *216*, 217
Ricotta Donuts, Lemon, *216*, 217
rising of dough, 12
Rocky Road Cookies, *30*, 31
rules of gluten-free baking, 12–13

S

Sandwich Cookies, Dark Chocolate, *26*, 27
Scones, Cranberry-Orange, *104*, 105
Scotcheroos, *114*, 115
Sherbet, Rainbow, 196, *197*
shortbread
Chocolate Shortbread Cookies, *42*, 43
Confetti Shortbread Cookies, *42*, 43
Shortcake Cookies, Strawberry, *18*, 19
Skillet Blueberry Crumble, *176*, 177
S'mores Brownies, 112, *113*
Soft Pretzels, 78, *79*
sorbet
Grapefruit Sorbet, 199
Lemon Sorbet, *184*, 199
Orange Sorbet, *198*, 199
Sour Cherry Pie, *4–5*, 162, *163*
Sourdough Bread, 101–102, *103*
Speedy Bagels, *74*, *94*, 95
Stone Fruit Galette, *160*, 161
strawberries
Chocolate-Covered Strawberry Macarons, *46*, 47
Strawberries & Cream Cake, *54*, 55
Strawberry Cheesecake Cupcakes, *132*, 133

strawberries (*continued*)
- Strawberry Shortcake Cookies, *18*, 19
- Strawberry Whip, *194*, 195

Strawberries & Cream Cake, *54*, 55
Strawberry Cheesecake Cupcakes, *132*, 133
Strawberry Macarons, Chocolate-Covered, *46*, 47
Strawberry Shortcake Cookies, *18*, 19
Strawberry Whip, *194*, 195
Stuffed Churros, 226–228, *227*
Stuffed Fluffernutter Cookies, 20, *21*
substitutions, 15
Sugar Cookie Bars, Frosted, *108*, 120, *121*
sugar cookies
- Sugar Cookie Bars, Frosted, *108*, 120, *121*
- Sugar Cookies, Cut-Out, 44, *45*

Sugar Cookies, Cut-Out, 44, *45*
sugar substitutions, 15
Sweet Potato Cinnamon Cupcakes, 150, *151*
Swirl Cheesecake, Raspberry, *68*, 69
Swirl Pumpkin Bread, Chocolate, *76*, 77

T

Tart, Frangipane Fruit, *164*, 165
Tart, Lemon Poppy Seed, *14*, *172*, 173
Tart, Red Wine Pear, 170, *171*
tarts
- Frangipane Fruit Tart, *164*, 165
- Lemon Poppy Seed Tart, *14*, *172*, 173
- Red Wine Pear Tart, 170, *171*

Tiramisu Trifle, *58*, 59–60
Trifle, Tiramisu, *58*, 59–60

U

Upside-Down Bananas Foster Cake, *64*, 65

V

vegan substitutions, 15

W

wheat starch, 11
Whip, Mango, *194*, 195
Whip, Pineapple, *194*, 195
Whip, Strawberry, *194*, 195
whipping ingredients, 13
White Cake Cupcakes, *144*, 145

Z

zucchini
- Zucchini Bread, *90*, 91
- Zucchini Cupcakes, Chocolate 146, *147*

Zucchini Bread, *90*, 91
Zucchini Cupcakes, Chocolate 146, *147*